SHOW US THE FATHER

*The Father's love for a lost
and fatherless generation*

Acknowledgements

I am so grateful to my husband Bob and my wonderful adult children for encouraging me to pursue my desire to write on this subject. Thank you for believing in me, giving practical suggestions and being available to contribute your own life stories to this book.

Thanks to all my special friends who agreed to read drafts of the book, and who have given positive feedback and spiritual insight and have inspired me to keep going on this journey of writing. I am so thankful for all your encouragement to finish what I started.

A big thank you to MyChurch Windsor, my spiritual family, for the huge impact that you have had on my life through friendship and support. Thank you Dr Sharon Stone and Greg Black for sharing your lives, as examples of spiritual mentorship to so many people. I respect you, and have received so much through your teaching and impartation. As leaders you have a vision to see people stand strong in their faith and be released into God-given giftings and callings. Thank you Dr Sharon for a prophetic word given in 2000, "It's like the Lord has given you such a creative side that has an expression in the area of writing. I've even raised up within you an ability to see some of the platforms given to those creative areas."

Thank you Helen Jones for your meticulous editorial skills and hard work, and for your invaluable patience in editing, proofreading, layout and book cover design.

SHOW US THE FATHER

Contents

SHOW US THE FATHER

Introduction

I was on a long-haul flight from Australia to London with a stopover at Doha. The connecting flight from Pakistan joined ours and we were ready to take off again, bound for Heathrow, London. As I sat next to a fellow passenger, he introduced himself and in conversation I said that I was a Christian. I showed him my copy of the New Testament and he began to read the preface, asking questions about the differences between the Old and New Testaments. He said that this was the first time he had ever held or read the Christian Bible. I explained that the Old Testament tells the history of the Jewish nation, and of the many prophets who foretold of Jesus Christ, the Messiah, who was to come. My fellow passenger recognized the names of the prophets, as they are also in his holy Qur'an.

I pointed to the verse in my New Testament that talks about the coming of Jesus Christ into the world. He read it out loud, but as he did so, he changed the wording and said, "For God so loved *the Christians* that He gave His only begotten Son that whoever believes in Him should not perish but have everlasting life." "No," I said. "For God so loved the *whole world* that He gave His only begotten Son," and the gift of everlasting life is for "whoever believes" (italics mine). [1] I then showed him the chapters that record the story of the death and resurrection of

---

1   John 3:16,17

SHOW US THE FATHER

Jesus Christ, the Son of God, the Saviour of the *whole world*.

Our conversation had the potential to be life changing for this middle-aged man as we flew over the place where Jesus was born in a stable nearly 2000 years ago. Never before had he heard what I was telling him. I sensed that he was deeply troubled by this revelation that had interrupted his normal thought pattern about the god that he had been brought up to believe in and prayed to all his life. Our dialogue was causing my travelling companion to question all the assumptions that he had probably taken for granted and accepted since childhood. In addition, he had most likely been taught not to question the truth of the deep traditions and sacred writings that had been passed down through the generations, originating from the place that we were now flying over. I offered him my New Testament as a gift, but he refused, instead saying that he would Google it.

I am writing for those of all faiths and religions, or those of no faith, who are uncertain about the future and even more so, life after death. Many people haven't thought of God as Father and are asking the fundamental question, "Is there really a God?" and "What is the meaning of life?" From the beginning to the end of the Bible, God reveals to us that He is Father. Then at the right time, God sent His Son Jesus into the world to die on the cross, taking the punishment for our sins so making it possible for us to have a relationship with God as Father. When Jesus was on earth, he made a promise to those who believe in Him. He said, "I am the way to the Father, I will not leave you orphans; I will come to you." [2] This message, even though spoken long ago, is still for us today, for those of any faith who choose to believe what the Bible says.

In our communities, there are many families where children are longing for the love of a father. I know of people who have no memory of their earthly dad, because they were separated at an early age, either physically or emotionally, or both. Sadly, I met an intelligent woman whose husband approached her for marriage so that he could apply for a UK passport, which he did. The marriage didn't last, and her son now has very little contact with his dad. This is a story that we often hear about in our modern society. In the 2021 census, just over fifteen per cent of families in the UK were lone parent families. [3] Our relationship with our earthly dad can affect the way we think about God as Father. The coming of Jesus Christ into the world brings hope to us and fills the gap in our empty hearts that longs for a father's love and kindness. When we open our hearts to Jesus the Son of God, we discover the Father who we can trust.

---

2   John 14:6,18

3   www.ons.gov.uk, Office for National Statistics, UK Census 2021

Part One:
PROLOGUE

1 Searching for the truth

"Ask, and it will be given to you; seek, and you will find; knock, and it will be opened to you. For everyone who asks receives, and he who seeks finds, and to him who knocks it will be opened." (Matthew 7:7,8)

The conversation that I had with my friend on the plane about the verses from the Gospel of John chapter 3 verse 16 was relevant for me too. I needed to read the Bible, and find out for myself about the God who is love, the Creator of the whole world and of Jesus Christ, the one who claimed to be the Son of God. When Jesus lived on earth, one of His disciples asked Him to, "show us the Father". [1] This question is still relevant today for all who are seeking to know the truth, including you and me.

When I was young, I learned about God, and longed to find out more about Him, but knowing God as a nurturing Father who loved me was outside my experience. I believed in God with my mind, but my heart knew that something was missing and there must be more. I didn't understand what life was all about and felt empty on the inside. As a family, we weren't taught to question and must accept what was modelled from our strict Protestant heritage. We routinely went to church twice on a Sunday, and read the Bible together as a family, discussing the correct Christian doctrine as well as learning

---

1   John 14:8

the catechisms by heart. The truth about religion was taught with deep conviction from those I respected. I mustn't reject it, because I honoured my father with his strong faith in God. But I was genuinely searching to know the creator God for myself, the great, holy God who was to be feared. What did it mean to have a personal faith in God, rather than religion that I'd inherited from previous generations?

Just because I had been brought up in a Christian family, didn't make me a Christian. Even as a child, I thought that there must be more to life than what I saw and heard in the world around me. Deep down I was frightened of the distant God in the sky who punished people. So knowing God as a loving, nurturing, personal Father never occurred to me; this possibility was beyond my reach.

Others who weren't brought up in a Christian family have a different experience of faith in Jesus Christ, like my daughter-in-law. She grew up in a home where God wasn't really mentioned, and she couldn't remember having any thoughts about His existence. Her childhood was secure, because she was made to feel loved by her exceptional mother but the relationship with an abusive dad was very difficult, and eventually her parents separated, leaving my daughter-in-law feeling insecure and broken. In her teens, she was taken to a church conference, where for the first time she heard about God in a new way. She felt at peace and more loved than she had ever been before. She heard God speaking directly to her, words of comfort and meaning. The voice of God said, "I am

Your Father and I love you more than you can fathom. I have never stopped loving you and I never will. I want to give you a new life and show you what a real Father's love looks like." At that moment, she felt that her whole life was transformed, and she was flooded with peace, joy and hope. She said, "I feel so cared for by God as my Father, who encourages me each day, and tells me that I have more worth than I can possibly imagine."

I had assumed that the only way to approach God was through the mind and not through the heart, because that was what I'd been taught. But my spiritual journey led to the discovery that knowing God who made the world is not about an intellectual discussion or having correct religious doctrine but about faith in His existence, and His love for us. The God of the Bible is all-powerful; He is everywhere and is interested in the hidden secrets of our lives. Each of us is loved and known by God. Before time began, we were in the mind of the Creator God and our uniqueness was there from the beginning.

At this point in my life, instead of allowing past fears and unbelief to control my thinking, or even memories of past religious arguments to remain alive, I began to seek this God who was protecting and guiding me and showing me what it means to know Him as a loving Father.

We read awe-inspiring words in the Bible that talk about God knowing every one of us before the world began, even before we were conceived in our mother's womb. This means that our identity was established before the beginning of time in the origins of creation.

Psalm 139 says, "You made all the delicate, inner parts of my body and knit me together in my mother's womb. Thank you for making me so wonderfully complex! Your workmanship is marvellous – how well I know it. You watched me as I was being formed in utter seclusion, as I was woven together in the dark of the womb. You saw me before I was born. Every day of my life was recorded in your book. Every moment was laid out before a single day had passed." [2]

It's easy *not* to believe what God is saying here, as we've let so many words spoken over us as children define our characters. I began by questioning any words that were not true, especially if they didn't agree with what God said about me. We are all important to God and He doesn't see us as stupid or a failure, so neither should we. The Bible says that God has a book, and every intimate detail of our daily lives is fashioned for us, and is written down in His book. Each of us is fearfully and wonderfully made and we are not a mistake.

God doesn't want us to get to the end of our life and for us to say that we never knew Him. Now is the time to begin this journey of knowing God. The key is to open our hearts to the truth that God made us and He is the perfect Dad, the One our natural father could never be. He is a good, good Father, pursuing us from the beginning of time, the One who loves us in the same way that He loves Jesus. He can be trusted.

---

2   Psalm 139:13-16 NLT

Part Two:
IN THE BEGINNING

2 And God said

How do we know God who is called Father? Who is the great God who made the world and everything in it? I was searching for answers to these questions, so I began by reading the story of creation, about how the world came into being. You can read about the mystery of creation in the first book of the Bible, Genesis chapters 1-3, which tell us in detail what happened on each day as God spoke. In the beginning there was no form and the world was empty and in complete darkness. [1]

It was here that the Spirit of God was 'hovering' or 'moving' over the face of the deep, just like a divine Artist standing before a blank canvas. In the beginning, God created the heavens and the earth and we read that this Creator God spoke! He *spoke* the world into being by the word of His mouth, and overcame darkness with light. "Then God said, 'Let there be light'; and there was light." [2]

As God spoke, there was a separation between day and night, and land from sea. The waters He called 'seas' and the dry land He called 'earth', that brought forth grass, herbs and fruit trees. He made the living creatures and birds, each according to their kinds. He made great lights to rule the day and night, called the sun and moon. [3] Other verses in the Old

---

1   Genesis 1:1,2
2   Genesis 1:3
3   Genesis 1:5-25

Testament tell us "The Lord merely spoke and the heavens were made. He breathed the word, and all the stars were born." [4] God was the One who stretched out the heavens with His hands, and He laid the foundation of the earth all by Himself. [5] The great God began creation all alone.

There are many descriptions of what happened in the beginning; for example the psalmist tells us about the heavens as "the work of Your fingers, the moon and the stars, which You have ordained." [6] And we read about God who flung the stars into space, individually counting them and calling them all by name. "He counts the number of the stars; He calls them all by name. Great is our Lord, and mighty in power; His understanding is infinite." [7] The Creator isn't a distant impersonal God but He speaks, breaths and works with His hands and fingers, just like us. God is a personal God. We live in His world. All the plant life, living creatures and everything that moves are the work of God's voice and His hands showing His personhood. Although the word 'Father' isn't actually mentioned in the Genesis story, we begin to understand His character.

God expressed pleasure and delight in all that He had made. The Bible says, "God saw that it was good … then God saw everything that he had made, and indeed it was very good." [8]

---

4   Psalm 33:6 NLT

5   Isaiah 44:24

6   Psalm 8:3

7   Psalm 147:4-5, Isaiah 40:26

8   Genesis 1:10,12,25,31

He was glad, and wants us to respond in the same way and to enjoy the beauty of His creation. But more than that, we take delight in God the Creator Himself. My religious mindset was being turned upside down as I found myself responding to colour, form, variety and even humour in what is made. The beauty of creation is overwhelming, from vast mountains to the detail and colour of tiny flowers. Just looking at the moon on a dark night was enough for me to believe in the existence of God. I realized that all creativity has its source in the God of Genesis. My emotions were awakened with delight and pleasure at the beauty of God's world.

Every living creature sings and claps alongside the Creator over creation, including the trees, the birds and the animals, as well as men and women. The Scripture describes this: "Let the trees of the forest sing for joy before the Lord." [9] "Let the field and their crops burst out with joy! Let the trees of the forest sing for joy." [10] "The mountains and hills will burst into song, and the trees of the field will clap their hands!" [11]

We can see what other people in the Old Testament say in order to understand more about the nature of God. The book of Job is one of the oldest books in the Bible, and in it Job asks questions in order to make the reader think. He suggests that we should ask the birds, the fish, the beasts of the field, and even the earth itself about the author of creation.

---

9   1 Chronicles 16:33 NLT
10   Psalm 96:12,13 NLT
11   Isaiah 55:12 NLT

"But now ask the beasts, and they will teach you;
And the birds of the air, and they will tell you;
Or speak to the earth, and it will teach you;
And the fish of the sea will explain to you.
Who among all these does not know
That the hand of the LORD has done this,
In whose hand is the life of every living thing,
And the breath of all mankind"[12]

Later on, the Lord God asks Job to consider:

"Has the rain a father?
Or who has begotten the drops of dew?
From whose womb comes the ice?
And the frost of heaven, who gives it birth?"[13]

Through these rhetorical questions we have an incredible insight into a paternal God who fathered all of creation and of the world being 'begotten' or brought to birth in the womb of a maternal Father. God as Father is One who speaks and who reasons; He even commands the hawk and the eagle to mount up and fly. [14]We can look with fresh eyes at every drop of rain, every blade of grass, the trees and the birds, all fathered by the Father of creation. Just as God creates beauty, colour, form and energy, and provides for the flowers of the field and the birds of the air, so He supplies all our needs.

In the New Testament, Jesus tells us to look beyond our

---

12   Job 12:7-10
13   Job 38:28,29
14   Job 39:26,27

daily worries about food and clothes and compare ourselves to the birds and the flowers. He says, "…do not worry about your life what you will eat or what you will drink; nor about your body, what you will put on. Look at the birds of the air … your heavenly Father feeds them. Are you not of more value than they?" God's care for the natural world also applies to us. He provides for all our needs just as He does for the birds of the air. In fact He says, "Are you not of more value than they?" [15]

When I needed to speak to my father as a child I would knock on his study door and he would say, "Come in!" It's not like that with God our Father. The whole of His creation is His office, and we don't have to knock on the door to get in. We can freely enter and speak to Him. He invites us to enjoy all that He has made – the beauty, the grandeur, the colours, the forms. His creation is where He walks with us and talks to us.

One day God spoke these words to me: "Don't underestimate the mystery of creation I, the Father, created. Come into the garden, my child; this is your home." Stepping into the garden, I discovered that the beauty of creation is overwhelming, and is about a God who is the Creator.

The history of creation continues in Genesis, when God said, "Let Us make man in Our image, according to Our likeness." [16] This is the first indication of the essence of who God is – He describes Himself in the plural, 'Us'. This doesn't mean that there is more than one God, but that there is

---

15 Matthew 6:25,26

16 Genesis 1:26

relationship within the Godhead. Just as we are made of three parts body, soul and spirit, so the 'Us' includes God as Creator, "the Spirit of God who hovered over the face of the water" that we read about at the beginning of the creation story, and Jesus the Son.

In Genesis 3 we read about the One who was to be born into the world through the offspring of Adam and Eve, described as the 'Seed' of Eve. [17] This is a prophecy pointing to the One who was to come, which was fulfilled many generations later through the birth of Jesus Christ, the offspring or 'son' of Adam described in the New Testament as the "Seed, who is Christ." [18] Jesus is also called the 'Word', who was in the beginning with God and who was God, through whom God spoke the world into being. Before creation, in the beginning, the triune God already existed in community as Father, Son and Spirit. You can read about the Word who was with God, and was God in the Gospel of John:

"In the beginning was the Word, and the Word was with God and the Word was God. He was in the beginning with God. All things were made through Him, and without Him nothing was made that was made ... as many as received Him, to them He gave the right to become children of God, to those who believe in His name." [19]

To summarize, we now know that when God said, "Let Us make man in Our image, according to Our likeness," God's

---

17 Genesis 3:15

18 Galatians 3:16

19 John 1:1-3,12

Spirit was active in creation, and the Word (Jesus) was with God, and was God, so all persons of God are in relationship within the Godhead. And we, who are made in His image are made after the likeness of a personal God.

God is a mystery, but John the author of John's Gospel, the disciple who was closest to Jesus, shows us that God is Father at work in creation, together with the 'Word', His Son. John says, "No one has seen God at any time. The only begotten Son, who is in the bosom of the Father, He has declared Him." And Jesus himself says "Not that anyone has seen the Father except He [Jesus] who is from God; He has seen the Father" (brackets mine). [20]So we see here that *no-one* has ever seen God the Father, but only Jesus the Son, who is from God.

---

20   John 1:18, 6:46 3.

3 Let Us make man

We read that on the sixth day of creation God said, "Let Us make man." Genesis 2 goes on to tell us "The LORD God formed man of the dust of the ground, and breathed into his nostrils the breath of life; and man became a living being." [1] One of the profound names of God is El Shaddai, meaning 'many breasted'. God as Father therefore has within Himself both a masculine and feminine identity and He formed man out of His own image. He created them both male and female and said, "Let Us make man in Our image, according to Our likeness; let them have dominion over ... all the earth ... God created man in His own image, in the image of God He created him; male and female He created them." [2]

So man was formed supernaturally after the essential nature of God Himself, and carries within himself all the attributes and character of God. God describes man, as made in 'Our image', according to 'Our likeness'. After God made Adam, He caused a deep sleep to fall on him and He took one of his ribs from which He made the woman, and brought her to Adam. He said, "It is not good for the man to be alone. I will make him a helper who is just right for him." [3] The first man and woman were formed after God's likeness or image for companionship and relationship, which we see reflects the

1   Genesis 2:7
2   Genesis 1:26,27
3   Genesis 2:18 NLT

relationship between Father, Son and Spirit. The Lord God planted a garden eastward of Eden, and there He put the man and woman whom He had made. God chose the earth as the habitation for mankind, the only planet where there is life.

Through the creation of man and woman, God is revealing to us our true identity; there is no confusion here. God formed man and woman from the dust of the earth – out of the dust came the beauty or pinnacle of His creation, formed in 'Our image' and made from the very nature of God Himself. We are made after His image with all the characteristics of male and female that are found in God. Every man and woman who has ever walked on this earth is made after the likeness of the eternal God, the One who thinks, knows and reasons, the One who feels and expresses pleasure. Remember that we are formed after the likeness of the eternal Father, fearfully and wonderfully made, in the likeness of God. Our identity is deeply rooted in the very nature of God Himself.

We can't question that God had a relationship with Adam, as Father and son. They walked through the Garden of Eden, enjoying each other company, talking together. God related to Adam and Eve as a Father to His children, "They heard the sound of the LORD God walking in the garden in the cool of the day." [4] Eden is believed nowadays to be located in the region of present-day Iraq.

Even though Adam isn't directly referred to as God's son in the Genesis story, we read in the New Testament about

---

4   Genesis 3:8

the historical genealogy of Jesus Christ starting with Adam, "the son of God". [5] So Adam is called the son of God; even though not born physically, he was the first man, created supernaturally by God from the dust of the earth. If Adam is recorded as being the son of God, so God is his Father.

When creation was complete, God expressed pleasure in His work. God, who made the world and everything in it, is One who speaks, and shows emotions as He expresses delight at the work of His hands. We too are made in His image, so emotions of joy and fulfilment are part of who we are. We know God through our emotional response to Him, and, as Father, He takes delight in His children.

Relationship originated in the heart of God the Father who had an unspoiled relationship with his son Adam before sin entered the world. Perfect unity between God and man was always intended to be as it was in the beginning where God's son, Adam, knew God as his Father in Paradise. Adam and Eve too were made for relationship with one another. There came a time, however, when Adam and Eve made wrong choices which spoiled their relationship with God as Father and also changed their relationship with one another. To understand why creation was spoiled, we need to look at the conversations that were going on in the garden.

---

5   Luke 3:23-38

4 The tree of life

I t's time to pause and ask the obvious question: "How can the story of creation as recorded in the Bible many centuries ago relate to me today?"

One day God the Father spoke clearly to me in a vision as He took me into the Garden of Eden and gave me fruit from the tree of life. In the vision, I ate the fruit and He said to me, "I give you the heart of sonship. You are no longer an orphan; you have the heart of my Son. No longer eat from the tree of knowledge of good and evil; eat from the tree of life."

The vision in the garden was another life-changing experience – God giving revelation of my true identity as His daughter. I needed to go back to Genesis 1–3 in order to find the Garden of Eden and to understand the significance of the tree of life that was in my vision and what it means to be sons and daughters.

The Genesis story continues. The Lord God planted a garden in Eden, and there He put the man whom he loved, the pinnacle of His creation, to work the garden and care for it. The Lord God made many beautiful trees out of the ground that were pleasant to look at and were a source of food for Adam and Eve. You can imagine God walking in the garden with Adam and Eve in perfect harmony, enjoying His creation. This was Paradise. Of the many trees that were in God's garden there were two trees that God pointed out: "The tree of life in the midst of the garden, and the tree of the knowledge of good and evil." [1]

There are many references to the tree of life running like a thread through the Bible from the book of Genesis to Revelation, showing the eternal significance of this tree. Death mustn't touch the tree of life. We read about the fruit from the tree of life, which is good to eat and gives life to all. All who eat of it shall be healed and live. In Proverbs, it says that the tree of life is a metaphor for Wisdom, "She is a tree of life to those who take hold of her, and happy are all who retain her", and "The fruit of the righteous is a tree of life." [2] Also right at the end of the Bible the tree of life, bearing fruit, is described as standing next to the pure river of life. Jesus speaks to the church and says "to him who overcomes, I will give to eat from the tree of life, which is in the midst of the Paradise of God." [3]

God loves trees! There were many trees in Eden, the perfect garden where Adam and Eve had complete freedom to eat the fruit of the trees, apart from one tree that was prohibited. [4] The tree of life stood in the middle of the garden, but there was another tree marked by God as important: this was the tree of the knowledge of good and evil. At first God tells Adam what he *can* do. He could eat from every tree in the garden, including the tree of life, the fruit of which was good to eat and gives life to all who eat of it.

---

1   Genesis 2:9
2   Proverbs 3:18; 11:30
3   Revelation 22:1,2; 2:7
4   Genesis 2:16,17; 1:29

But Adam and Eve were forbidden to eat or even touch the tree of the knowledge of good and evil, in the middle of the garden. The Lord God spoke to Adam and for the first time gave him an important command: "Of every tree of the garden you may freely eat, but of the tree of the knowledge of good and evil you shall not eat, for in the day that you eat of it you shall surely die." [5]

This was the line beyond which the man, Adam, must not cross. The possibility of death lay within the Garden of Eden. At this point, we read of evil appearing in the garden in the form of a serpent who speaks and challenges Eve to eat fruit from the tree of the knowledge of good and evil. But Eve replies by repeating what God had said. "We may eat the fruit of the trees of the garden; but of the fruit of the tree which is in the midst of the garden, God has said, 'You shall not eat it, nor shall you touch it, lest you die.'" [6]

The tree of the knowledge of good and evil would lead to death. All who eat of this tree shall surely die. So, here we see that God tells Adam and Eve what they can and can't do; they were given freedom of choice. The command not to eat of this tree was the first time God gave man a choice. Every human being has the liberty to choose between right and wrong, good and evil, and it began in the Garden of Eden. Adam was told not to eat or even touch the tree of the knowledge of good and evil, in the middle of the garden. Obedience to God

---

5   Genesis 2:16.17

6   Genesis 3:2,3

meant that Adam would stay in relationship with the Father as His son, but a wrong choice would lead to the breakdown of that relationship. If Adam ate from this tree, he would die spiritually, and death would pass to the whole world. The consequence of sin is death.

The day came when Adam and Eve were tempted by the serpent to eat the forbidden fruit from the wrong tree, and, as they ate, Adam and Eve took into themselves the seed of sin. "So when the woman saw that the tree was good for food, that it was pleasant to the eyes, and a tree desirable to make one wise, she took of its fruit and ate. She also gave to her husband with her, and he ate. Then the eyes of both of them were opened, and they knew that they were naked." [7]

Unity between Adam and Eve, and with God the Father, was broken and spoiled as a shadow passed over the Garden of Eden and death entered the world. Instead of drawing close to God as Father as they had known, Adam and Eve withdrew from God, and covered themselves with leaves in order to hide, because they were ashamed. They heard the voice of the Lord God in the garden, and for the first time the relationship with God as their Father was spoiled. Adam said, "I heard Your voice in the garden, and I was afraid because I was naked; and I hid myself." [8] But it is impossible to hide from God.

At this point in the history of the world, Adam and Eve became orphaned and guilt entered their hearts, which was

---

7   Genesis 3:6,7
8   Genesis 3:10

something they had never known before. Shame and fear followed as a result of their guilt, all signs of an orphan spirit which had now entered the human race. And like all orphans, Adam and Eve felt abandoned.

Is this narrative relevant to you and me today? The answer is a resounding "Yes!" The historical reality of Adam and Eve's disobedience caused sin to be imparted to the human race. We all carry within us the orphan spirit because Genesis chapters 1–3 reveal to us the origins of sin and consequent separation from God as Father. In the Garden of Eden, God gave Adam and Eve the freedom to choose between good and evil and to have dominion over the created world but instead they ate from the tree of the knowledge of good and evil, and so walked away from knowing God as Father and became orphaned. Through their wrong choice, death entered the human race and consequently Paradise was spoiled. The Lord drove those he loved out of Paradise, from the presence of their Father, in order to protect the tree of life.

"'And now, lest he [Adam] put out his hand and take also of the tree of life, and eat, and live forever' – therefore the Lord God sent him out of the garden of Eden to till the ground from which he was taken. So He drove out the man; and He placed cherubim at the east of the garden of Eden, and a flaming sword which turned every way, to guard the way to the tree of life" (brackets mine). [9]

---

9   Genesis 3:22-24

5. Are there really two fathers?

What do we know about the serpent who spoke to Eve in the Garden of Eden? We don't have all the answers, but there is evidence that Satan was cunning and disguised himself as a serpent. In Genesis 1–3 we hear two voices speaking to Adam and Eve in the garden. Firstly, there was God the Father who spoke truth, and secondly the serpent, who misinterpreted the truth. The serpent was "made by God", as the account tells us "he was more cunning than any beast of the field which the Lord God had made." [1]

The beguiling snake spoke an element of truth but not the whole truth. He mixed truth with lies and questioned God's words by asking Eve whether God "had really said" that she may not eat of every tree in the garden? Then he twisted the truth and added his own interpretation, by telling Eve "You will not surely die. For God knows that in the day you eat of it your eyes will be opened, and you will be like God, knowing good and evil." [2] The truth is that God *had* said to Adam and Eve "in the day that you eat of it you shall surely die". [3] However, Adam wanted to be like God, so he listened to the serpent, the father of pride, who deceived him into eating fruit from the wrong tree. We don't know whether the serpent himself ate from the tree of the knowledge of good and evil before Adam and Eve,

---

1   Genesis 3:1
2   Genesis 3:4,5
3   Genesis 2:17

but the Bible does say that Satan wanted to be like God. His words to Eve "if you eat of the fruit of this tree you will be like God" show his desire, if not his experience. Had the serpent eaten from this tree; had his eyes already been opened to the knowledge of good and evil?

Two Old Testament prophets in particular write about the ancient serpent, the deceiver, who exalted himself to be like God. Isaiah gives a detailed description of Satan or Lucifer, "you are fallen from heaven … for you have said in your heart: 'I will ascend into heaven, I will exalt my throne above the stars of God … I will be like the Most High.'" [4]

Ezekiel also talks about what the prince of Tyre is like, but his words have a double meaning as he is also referring to Satan – the visible and the invisible. The pride of the human prince is described like this: "your heart is lifted up and you say, 'I am a god, I sit in the seat of gods … you set your heart as the heart of a god… '" But there is also a hidden reference to Satan, "you were … full of wisdom and perfect in beauty. You were in Eden, the garden of God … you were perfect in your ways from the day you were created, till iniquity was found in you … your heart was lifted up because of your beauty; you corrupted your wisdom for the sake of your splendour." [5]

Back in the Garden of Eden, we read that Adam and Eve listened to the lie and disobeyed God by eating the fruit of the tree of the knowledge of good and evil as the way to be like

---

4   Isaiah 14:12-14
5   Ezekiel 28:1-17

God. This was the first time that Adam had been lied to. Adam and Eve *did* want to be like God the Father so listened to the wrong voice and partial truth. By doing so, the relationship with God was spoiled and broken. Orphans don't know who their earthly father is, or their heavenly Father, and they live in fear and shame and are comfortless, just as Adam and Eve were. Through Satan, the orphan spirit entered the world. Satan was the ultimate orphan.

Adam and Eve were distanced from God and became orphaned, just like Satan, no longer wanting to be in the presence of their Father, nor able to hear His voice. Instead, they withdrew and hid. Orphans are separated from fathers because of rejection and shame, which is the opposite of relationship. When Adam and Eve were driven from the garden, they left behind them the knowledge of God as Father, and so shame, fear and the orphan spirit entered the world for the first time. The deception first came from Satan who was the original orphan, no longer in relationship with the God whom he had originally known. Instead of listening to the voice of God, Adam and Eve opened their hearts to the orphan spirit by listening to the voice of the first orphan, who was the father of lies.

The same two voices challenge us today, and we have to discern which is speaking the truth. We must ask ourselves, which voice we are going to listen to and obey. In the New Testament, Jesus tells us about the counterfeit father, the father of lies who tempts us to follow him. Jesus, by contrast, affirms His true identity as the Son of God – in declaring this He offended the religious leaders of the day. He tells them that He only speaks the truth, which He has heard from His Father.

"He who believes in Me, believes not in Me but in Him who sent Me. And he who sees Me sees Him who sent Me. I have not spoken on my own authority; but the Father who sent Me gave Me a command, what I should say and what I should speak." [6]

We learn about the other father who Jesus speaks about as He challenges his opponents, the religious teachers and says, "I speak what I have seen with My Father, and you do what you have seen with your father [Satan]" (brackets mine). [7] Here we see there are two fathers: God, the Father of truth and Satan, the father of lies. Jesus revealed the true identity of the devil :

"You are of your father the devil … He was a murderer from the beginning, and does not stand in the truth, because there is no truth in him. When he speaks a lie, he speaks from his own resources, for he is a liar and the father of it." [8]

The devil speaks from his own character. Its important that we know Jesus, who is Truth.

We can read about another occasion when Satan directly tries to usurp Jesus' authority as the Son of God by tempting Jesus to submit to his [Satan's] power. Jesus is about thirty years old, ready to start His public ministry, but Satan tries to undermine Him. Satan quotes Old Testament scripture

---

6   John 12:44,45,49
7   John 8:38
8   John 8:44

but adds his own twisted interpretation. Satan shows Jesus all the kingdoms of the world, and wrongly claims an authority that has been given to him (Satan) with a direct disregard for truth. He confronts Jesus three times about His claim to be the Son of God. Satan says, "…if you are the Son of God, worship before me and all will be Yours." Jesus replies, "Get behind Me, Satan! For it is written, 'You shall worship the LORD your God, and Him only you shall serve.'" [9]

In the last book of the Bible, Satan's true identity is fully exposed, as "that serpent of old, called the Devil and Satan, who deceives the whole world". [10]

My friends, just as Adam and Eve had a choice in the Garden of Eden, so we face the same choice today. Do we listen to the Father of truth or do we follow evil and walk away from God just as Adam and Eve did? The orphan spirit strives to please God, and earn a place in Paradise, trying to reach God by living a life of good, religious deeds. The truth is that we can't please God by achievement. No matter how much we strive, we will always fall short of His standards. It's not by our man-made effort that we will please God, but by believing in what He's already done for us. He died on the cross to forgive us all our sins of unbelief and He offers us the free gift of eternal life which we can never earn. The only way to come to God is by faith in Jesus Christ, because He says, "I am the way, the truth, and the life. No one comes to the Father

---

9   Luke 4:1-13
10   Revelation 12:9

except through Me." [11] The Father receives us as His sons and daughters unconditionally, without us having to earn His love.

Adam's disobedience had a direct effect not only on mankind but also on the created world resulting in death and decay. Creation is waiting and longing for the redemption of sons and daughters as we believe in and worship the true, living Father. This is what sons and daughters are made for. When we come back into relationship with God our Father through Jesus Christ His Son, the whole of creation will be restored. The Bible describes creation groaning and labouring like a woman in childbirth to be "delivered from the bondage of corruption" as it "eagerly waits for the revealing of the sons of God". [12]

---

11 John 14:6
12 Romans 8:19-23

Part Three: RESTORATION

6 Fatherhood in the Old Testament

Fatherhood and family began in the heart of God and there are many stories of fathering that we can learn about from Jewish history in the Old Testament. It all starts with the commandment that God gave to the nation of Israel, "Honour your father and mother." [1]

The image of God as Father is described repeatedly in the Bible. God is the protector of the fatherless and the defender of the lost and the damaged, the helper of the orphan and the widow. "As a father pities his children, so the Lord pities those who fear Him." [2] And God is "a father of the fatherless, a defender of widows". [3] There is also an image of God covering and protecting us like a mother hen her chicks, "He shall cover you with His feathers and under His wings you shall take refuge." [4]

Most of all there is a strong biblical principle about mercy, compassion and justice for the weak and the vulnerable which is so relevant to us today. The Lord tells us to, "Execute true justice, show mercy and compassion everyone to his brother. Do not oppress the widow or the fatherless, the alien or the poor." [5]

Many biblical characters show us that family and marriage

---

1   Exodus 20:12
2   Psalm 103:13
3   Psalm 68:5
4   Psalm 91:4
5   Zechariah 7:9,10

are central to God's heart of fatherly love for humanity. When God created Adam and Eve, He made them as fully grown human beings and gave them the command to "Be fruitful and multiply; fill the earth." [6] So Adam and Eve became the first father and mother of the human race. And God said, "A man shall leave his father and mother and be joined to his wife, and they shall become one flesh." [7]

Job

The story of Job and his family of seven sons and three beautiful daughters is one of the earliest records of fathering in the Old Testament. Job, an honourable and upright man was also a spiritual father and counsellor to the needy. As well as caring for his own family, he protected the fatherless and those who were outcasts; he was a father to the poor and men listened to his counsel. "I delivered the poor who cried out, the fatherless and the one who had no helper ... I was a father to the poor." [8]

Abraham

Abraham was chosen by God to be the father of all nations. God spoke to Abraham and made a covenant with him to become the father not only of Israel, but also of many nations. [9]

He was called by God to leave his own country and his

---

6   Genesis 1:28
7   Genesis 2:24
8   Job 29:12,16
9   Genesis 12:2; 17:3,4

father's house and go to the land of Canaan and by doing so God promised to bless him and through him *all* the families of the earth would be blessed.

The patriarch gave birth to two sons, Ishmael and Isaac, but Isaac was the son of promise, and through him Abraham became the father of many nations, for all those who believe, both Jew and Gentile. Abraham's fatherhood and obedience to all the promises spoken over him were tested when he offered his son Isaac as a sacrifice on the altar before God. However, just before Abraham took his knife to kill Isaac, the Lord spoke clearly to him and said, "Do not lay your hand on the lad, or do anything to him; for now I know that you fear God, since you have not withheld your son, your only son from Me … in your seed all the nations of the earth shall be blessed, because you have obeyed My voice." [10]

Abraham's wife Sarah gave birth to Isaac at the age of ninety, and the Lord said of Sarah, "I will bless her … and she shall be a mother of nations." [11]

Israel

God had a personal relationship with the nation of ancient Israel, just as a father has with his son. Jacob (re-named Israel) was the grandson of Abraham. He fathered twelve sons, through whom came the twelve tribes of Israel. God as Father referred to the children of Israel as "His firstborn

---

10   Genesis 22:12,18; Romans 4:11,16-22
11   Genesis 17:16

son", the first of all nations through whom God would speak to many other nations. "Israel is My son, My firstborn ... let My son go that he may serve Me." [12] As the Israelites wandered in the wilderness, grumbling and complaining to Moses, he repeatedly challenges them not to *forget* the Father from whom they were formed. "Is He not your Father, who bought you... have [you] forgotten the God who fathered you?" [13]

The prophet Isaiah also reminds the Israelites not to forget God their Father: "the Lord who made you and formed you from the womb ... Israel whom I have chosen." [14] In reverse, Isaiah calls out to God, and reminds Him that He is Father, "Doubtless, You are our Father ... You, O LORD, are our Father ... Our Redeemer from Everlasting is Your name." [15] In other words, God our Father is from Everlasting: He existed before the world began.

In the same way, we need constantly reminding of our relationship with God as our Father. God isn't a distant, unapproachable God in the sky, but a loving, compassionate Father.

Isaiah also talks about the maternal nature of God, describing Him as a compassionate mother: "Can a woman forget her nursing child, and not have compassion on the son of her womb? Surely they may forget, yet I will not forget you.

---

12   Exodus 4:22,23
13   Deuteronomy 32:6,18
14   Isaiah 44:2
15   Isaiah 63:16

See, I have inscribed you on the palms of My hands." [16]

As a potter, I relate to the metaphor of God being like a potter, at the potter's wheel. The clay is soft, wet and malleable in the potter's hands as he moulds the clay, pressing and pulling. So God, the master Potter holds us in His hands, remoulding and refashioning His children, calling us back into relationship with Himself: "You are our Father; we are the clay, and You are our potter; and all we are the work of Your hand." [17]

The heart of the Father is one of abundant love and compassion. He reassures us through the prophets that He is Father. Jeremiah calls those who are backsliding in their faith to repent and return to the Lord. "You shall call me, 'My Father,' and not turn away from Me." [18] God even rebukes His people for making and worshipping idols. One example is where the Israelites would say to a tree, "You are my father", or to a stone, "You gave birth to me". [19] God speaks to us today through the Bible just as He spoke to the Israelites. He says, "Don't turn away from Me, don't reject Me."

We read about God's tender mercy and patience as a Father towards Israel. He heals their backsliding and loves the prodigals extravagantly. He speaks through the prophet Hosea, "I will heal their backsliding, I will love them freely." [20] There is a beautiful

---

16 Isaiah 49:15,16
17 Isaiah 64:8
18 Jeremiah 3:19,22
19 Jeremiah 2:27
20 Hosea 14:4

picture of God's fatherly love expressed by Him bending down and teaching the people to walk and by taking them in His arms. These words, even though spoken many years ago to ancient Israel, apply also to us:

> "When Israel was a child, I loved him … I called My son … I taught Ephraim to walk, taking them by their arms; but they did not know that I healed them. I drew them with gentle cords, with bands of love, and … I stooped down and fed them." [21]

Joseph

Joseph was the son of Jacob, the great-grandson of Abraham, born to Rachel. This is a family blessed with a generational legacy of fatherhood even though Joseph was rejected by his eleven brothers and sold into slavery. You can read the whole story in Genesis. [22] He prospered and was favoured within the Egyptian household of Pharaoh, and Joseph became not only lord of all Pharaoh's house, and ruler throughout the land of Egypt, but he became a spiritual *father* to Pharaoh himself. This is a story of an earthly father's love, and also what it means to be a spiritual father. "[God] has made me a father to Pharaoh, and lord of all his house, and a ruler throughout the land of Egypt." [23]

---

21 Hosea 11:1-4
22 Genesis 37 – 50
23 Genesis 45:8

Ruth

The book of Ruth in the Bible tells us that many years ago a young Moabite woman, Ruth, left her own family and pagan religion and followed her Jewish mother-in-law, Naomi, to Bethlehem in the land of Judah. Ruth, even though a Gentile, trusted Naomi her spiritual mother, as they built a new life together. Ruth said, "Your people shall be my people, and your God, my God." [24] She left her own family roots and joined herself with the God of Israel. But God had even bigger ideas. Many generations later, Jesus Christ, whose lineage is traced to David, the great-great-grandson of Ruth, was born in the same town. [25]

Esther

Esther was a young, orphaned Jewish girl who was given a home by her uncle Mordecai. [26] As her adopted father, Mordecai nurtured and cared for Esther as his own daughter. She then 'left' Mordecai in order to follow the true God and fulfil her own spiritual destiny of marriage to the King, and consequent exposure of the plot to annihilate the Jewish race. In a role reversal, Mordecai as 'father' honoured Esther, as queen. "Mordecai went his way and did according to all that Esther commanded him." [27]

---

24 Ruth 1:16,17
25 Matthew 1:1-6; Luke 3:23-38
26 Esther 2:7
27 Esther 4:17

Samuel

The child prophet Samuel was dedicated to the Lord and given to Eli the priest who 'fathered' and mentored him in the Temple, teaching him to discern the voice of the Lord as distinct from the voice of his 'adopted father'. Sometimes God does speak through a mentor but the important principle in mentoring is to always discern what God is saying to you. This story can be found in 1 Samuel chapter 3.

Prophecy of Malachi

The book of Malachi is the last book of the Old Testament, written 430 years before the coming of Christ. This is the link between loss of fatherhood in the Garden of Eden and the New Testament restoration of fatherhood. Malachi prophesies of the coming of Elijah the prophet, speaking of John the Baptist, the one who would prepare the way for the coming of Jesus Christ and his foretelling of the restoration of fatherhood. "And he [John the Baptist] will turn the hearts of the fathers to the children, And the hearts of the children to their fathers" (brackets mine). [28]

---

28   Malachi 4:5,6

7 Old Testament prophecies fulfilled

The sign of a true prophet is that their words come to pass and this is exactly what happened to many of the Old Testament prophets. Over 300 Old Testament prophecies foretold the coming of the Messiah, with aspects of the birth of the Son of God, His ministry and miracles, death and resurrection fulfilled many hundreds of years after they were first spoken, many of which were quoted by the Prophet Jesus Christ Himself. Looking at the fulfilment of these prophecies confirms to us the truth of Scripture, and the overall plan of redemption fulfilled through the coming of Christ the Messiah.

Isaiah prophesied about John the Baptist, the prophet who was to come approximately 700 years later as a forerunner, the one who was to prepare the way of the Lord, "The voice of one crying in the wilderness: 'Prepare the way of the LORD; make straight in the desert a highway for our God.'" [1] John the Baptist himself spoke of the Messiah who was soon to come when he appeared in the wilderness, and was asked by the religious leaders whether he (John the Baptist) was the Christ or a prophet or Elijah, "Who are you?" they said. John the Baptist replied, quoting the prophet Isaiah, "[I am] the voice of one crying in the wilderness: make straight the way of the Lord,' as the prophet Isaiah said." [2]

---

1   Isaiah 40:3
2   John 1:23

Isaiah prophesied also of the virgin who would conceive, and of the babe to be born whose name means God with us:

"Behold the virgin shall conceive and bear a Son, and shall call His name Immanuel. Curds and honey He shall eat, that He may know to refuse the evil, and choose the good." [3] The fulfilment came when the angel Gabriel spoke to Joseph about the baby to be born to Mary, "And she will bring forth a Son, and you shall call His name Jesus, for He will save His people from their sins."

So all this was done that it might be fulfilled which was spoken by the Lord through the prophet [Isaiah], saying: "Behold, the virgin shall be with child, and bear a Son, and they shall call His name Immanuel," which is translated, "God with us" (brackets mine). [4]

The ancient prophet tells us that Jesus the Messiah would work miracles, and set the captives free. He would bind up the brokenhearted, give sight to the blind, and bring good news to the poor.

This is exactly what happened through the life of Jesus. One Sabbath day, Jesus went into the synagogue and He was handed the book of the prophet Isaiah. He stood up and read Isaiah's prophecy, which He Himself came to fulfil,

"The Spirit of the Lord is upon Me,
Because He has anointed Me

---

3   Isaiah 7:14,15
4   Matthew 1:21,22,23

To preach the gospel to the poor;
He has sent Me to heal the broken hearted,
To proclaim liberty to the captives
And recovery of sight to the blind,
To set at liberty those who are oppressed;
To proclaim the acceptable year of the Lord."

Then He closed the book and gave it back to the attendant and sat down. And the eyes of all who were in the synagogue were fixed on Him. And He began to say to them, 'Today this Scripture is fulfilled in your hearing.' [5]

Another prophesy about Jesus, the babe to be born, predicts that the town of Bethlehem would be the birthplace of Jesus Christ, the One who will rule forever:

"Bethlehem Ephrathah,
Though you are little among the thousands of Judah,
Yet out of you shall come forth to Me
The One to be ruler in Israel,
Whose goings forth are from of old,
From everlasting." [6]

Micah's prophesy is fulfilled when Herod who was the king at the time of Jesus' birth asked where the Christ was to be born. The religious leaders answered and said to him that the child would be born in Bethlehem,

---

5   Luke 4:16-21
6   Micah 5:2

"for thus it is written by the prophet [Micah]:

'But you, Bethlehem, in the land of Judah,

Are you not least among the rulers of Judah ;

For out of you shall come a Ruler

Who will shepherd My people Israel.' " (brackets mine).[7]

The writer in Psalms looks ahead to Jesus who would teach us in parables, "Incline your ears to the words of my mouth. I will open my mouth in a parable; I will utter dark sayings of old." [8]

Matthew, one of Jesus' disciples, quotes the prophecy in Psalms, which is to be fulfilled through Jesus:

"Jesus spoke to the multitude in parables; and without a parable He did not speak to them, that it might be fulfilled which was spoken by the prophet [Micah] saying: 'I will open My mouth in parables; I will utter things kept secret from the foundation of the world'" (brackets mine). [9]

Many detailed prophecies about the death and resurrection of Jesus were spoken centuries before Christ was born. There is the beautiful story in Matthew's Gospel of Jesus riding into Jerusalem on a donkey before His death, and the people cried out, "this is Jesus, the prophet from Nazareth of Galilee." [10] This was the fulfilment of words spoken by the prophet Zechariah many years previously,

---

7   Matthew 2:4-6

8   Psalm 78:1,2

9   Matthew 13:34-35

10   Matthew 21:11

"Behold your King is coming to you;
He is just and having salvation,
Lowly and sitting on a donkey,
A colt, the foal of a donkey." [11]

There is the historical record of the children of Israel complaining as they wandered in the wilderness following their exodus from Egypt. The Lord sent serpents among the people to bite them as punishment for their sins and He said to Moses the prophet, "Make a fiery serpent, and set it on a pole; and it shall be that everyone who is bitten, when he looks at it, shall live." [12] The fulfilment of this prophecy happened when Jesus describes the bronze pole as a symbol of His own death on the cross, "And as Moses lifted up the serpent in the wilderness, even so must the Son of Man be lifted up, that whoever believes in Him should not perish but have eternal life." [13]

At Jesus' death, His disciples abandoned Him but worse than that was his abandonment by the Father. As the psalmist prophesies, "My God, My God, why have You forsaken Me? Why are You so far from helping Me?" [14]

This was fulfilled when Jesus was on the cross; there was darkness over all the land, and at about the ninth hour, Jesus cried out with a loud voice, "My God, My God, why have You forsaken Me?" [15]

---

11   Matthew 21:4,5
12   Numbers 21:8
13   John 3:14,15
14   Psalm 22:1
15   Matthew 27:46

Isaiah 53 is a profound prophetic description of the suffering of Christ:

"He is despised and rejected by men, a Man of sorrows and acquainted with grief ... Surely He has borne our griefs and carried our sorrows ... But He was wounded for our transgressions, He was bruised for our iniquities; the chastisement for our peace was upon Him, and by His stripes we are healed ... He had done no violence, nor was any deceit in His mouth." [16]

Matthew also describes the suffering of Christ, demonstrating the fulfilment of the words spoken by Isaiah, "He Himself took our infirmities and bore our sicknesses." [17] And the disciple Peter also quotes Isaiah when he talks of the Christ who suffered for our iniquities, "Who committed no sin, nor was deceit found in His mouth" and "by whose stripes you were healed". [18]

These prophecies foretell with accurate detail the birth, the life, death and resurrection of Jesus Christ, fulfilled many years later. We have to take seriously these claims, based on century-old historical facts all pointing to the baby Jesus born in Bethlehem, the Saviour of the world who claimed to be the Son of God.

---

16   Isaiah 53:3,4,5,9
17   Matthew 8:17
18   1 Peter 2:22,24

Part Four:
REVELATION

8 Jesus came

"My Father has entrusted everything to Me. No one truly knows the Son except the Father, and no one truly knows the Father except the Son and those to whom the Son chooses to reveal Him." (Luke 10:22 NLT)

The birth of Jesus

The ancient prophecies telling of the birth of Jesus Christ, God's Son, were all fulfilled at exactly the right time and in the right place – the greatest event that changed the course of human history. We can read in detail about the young virgin engaged to be married, who conceived not in a natural way, but supernaturally. There was much angelic activity surrounding this timely birth, and the angel Gabriel visited Mary and said to her,

> "'Do not be afraid, Mary ... You will conceive in your womb and bring forth a Son and shall call His name JESUS. He will be great, and will be called the Son of the Highest ...' Then Mary said to the angel, 'How can this be, since I do not know a man?' And the angel answered and said to her, 'The Holy Spirit will come upon you and the power of the Highest will overshadow you; therefore also, that Holy One who is to be born will be called the Son of God' ... And she brought forth her firstborn Son

and wrapped Him in swaddling cloths, and laid Him in a manger, because there was no room for them in the inn." [1]

When Jesus was born, there was such jubilation – the angels sang and everyone in heaven gave Jesus a standing ovation. The noise was deafening – the joyful sound of praise and worship as He made His entrance on earth. The shepherds out on the hills saw a multitude of angels praising God, and they went quickly to find the babe lying in a manger. [2] God the Father sent Jesus as an infant into a humble stable. What a contradiction. Jesus, King of kings and Lord of heaven and earth made His entrance in humble surroundings. This was His beginning on earth. So we must never underestimate humble surroundings. However poor our home, the riches of heaven dwell there. Life is full of contradictions. Jesus came to earth with a mission. He was sent – the sent One.

Jesus Christ came to bring life to a lost world from the eternal consequences of sin, that is death, that originated in the Garden of Eden, and, through His death on the cross, death and Satan are defeated and relationship with the Father is restored. "For as the Father raises the dead and gives life to them, even so the Son gives life to whom He will." [3] On two occasions in the New Testament God's voice is heard from heaven affirming Jesus Christ as His beloved Son, "This is My beloved Son, in whom I am well pleased." [4]

1   Luke 1:30-35; 2:7
2   Luke 2:8-14
3   John 5:21
4   Matthew 3:17; 17:1-9; 2 Peter 1:17

Who is Jesus?

Look at the story in John's Gospel about Jesus choosing to reveal His identity to a Samaritan woman at a well, and asking her for a drink. Jews didn't normally have dealings with Samaritans, especially as she was a woman. Jesus then told the woman all she had ever done, and she recognized that he was a prophet. The woman, like many other people of the time knew that the Messiah, who is called the Christ, was coming, and she said, "when He comes He will tell us all things". Jesus then said to her "I who speak to you am He." The woman believed that this was indeed "the Christ, the Saviour of the world". Many of the Samaritans in that city believed in Him because of the testimony of the woman, "Come see a Man who told me all things that I ever did. Could this be the Christ?" [5] The coming of Jesus is life changing for *all* who believe.

I too had an encounter with Jesus but this was in the form of a vision. I was due to have surgery, so needed to be in complete isolation for two weeks before going to the hospital because of the infectious nature of a virus that was spreading globally. There was plenty of time to think, pray and wait all alone. Eventually the day came and, as I woke, I saw two very tall figures in long, white garments standing next to each other near the window of my bedroom. I wondered whether they were angels, but they seemed to be one person. Then I saw the words I AM. One figure was 'I' and the other 'AM', joined together as one person. 'I AM' stayed with me all day as I had surgery. They never left me.

---

5   John 4:1-42

When Jesus lived on earth about 2000 years ago, on one occasion the religious authorities challenged Him: "Who do you think you are?" Jesus replied, "I say to you, before Abraham was, I AM." [6] Because of Jesus' reply, the Jewish leaders, who claimed to be sons of Abraham, picked up stones to throw at Him, because they knew that He was declaring that He was equal with God, I AM being the name that God used of Himself. [7]

Jesus came to declare to the world His relationship with His Father. A clue to the nature of Father and Son is that they both carry life in themselves. "The Father has life in Himself, and He has also granted the Son to have life in Himself." [8] Jesus makes another profound statement, using the words I AM when speaking about Himself: "I am the resurrection and the life. He who believes in Me though he may die, he shall live. And whoever lives and believes in Me shall never die." [9] Jesus says the same thing to you and me, "Whoever hears My words and believes in Me, has the gift of everlasting life."

Relationship with the Father is restored

The tree of life that was planted in the Garden of Eden, is the same Jesus who declared, "I am the resurrection and the life", and all who believe in Jesus will live. We are invited to come and feed on Him. The tree of life is everlasting, and many

---

6   John 8:53-58
7   Exodus 3:14
8   John 5:26
9   John 11:25,26

throughout the world have eaten from this tree and will go on eating from it. Jesus tells us that He carries life in Himself: "As the living Father sent Me, and I live because of the Father, so he who feeds on Me will live because of Me." [10] Jesus came to show us the Father and He continues to reveal the Father's love now and for many generations to come.

Jesus was 'sent' into the world to restore what was lost in the Garden of Eden. Compare the consequences of Adam's disobedience and Christ's obedience:

"Just as through one man [Adam] sin entered the world, and death through sin ... even so through one Man's [Jesus] righteous act the free gift came to all men ... For as by one man's disobedience many were made sinners, so also by one Man's obedience many will be made righteous" (brackets mine).[11]

In the New Testament the Aramaic word for Father, Abba (ab'-bah), is used which means Pappa or Daddy. [12] He is our heavenly Father, our 'daddy'. This word shows the intimacy between the Father and His Son. "I have declared to them Your name, and will declare it", which means He goes on showing us the name of the Father, "that the love with which You loved Me may be in them, and I in them". [13] What a profound truth – Jesus continues to reveal the Father's love to each of us and

10 John 6:57

11 Romans 5:12-19

12 www.dictionary.com Roget's 21st Century Thesaurus Third edition, Copyright @ 2013 by the Philip Lief Group

13 John 17:26

it's the same love that God has for His Son. By receiving this love, our identity is affirmed as children of God, "I will be a Father to you, and you shall be My sons and daughters, says the LORD Almighty." [14]

Jesus is the way

When Jesus came to earth, He came with a mission. He was sent by God to reveal the Father's love to the world. Jesus talks about Himself as being the only way to the Father. No one can come to God the Father except through Jesus. Many people believe in Jesus as Saviour, because He is kind and loving whereas God as Father feels distant and unapproachable, the God in the sky who punishes. But Jesus came to show us the Father. The whole object of His coming was to make a way for us to come to the Father.

There's a key in John's Gospel that tells us about *the way* to come to the Father. Jesus clearly says "I am the way, the truth, and the life. No one comes to the Father except through Me." [15] It is so easy to stop after the first phrase "I am the way" without finding out the destination – where is Jesus leading us? What's the purpose for His coming? The journey isn't complete without the rest of the verse. Jesus is the *way* to the Father. "No-one comes to the Father except through me." Jesus is showing us the way to the Father *and* also the way to the Father's house, because He is the way. Philip's request to Jesus is the same as ours:

---

14   2 Corinthians 6:18
15   John 14:6

"Philip said to Him, 'Lord, show us the Father, and it is sufficient for us.' Jesus said to him, 'Have I been with you so long, and yet you have not known Me Philip? He who has seen Me has seen the Father; so how can you say "show us the Father"? Do you not believe that I am in the Father, and the Father in Me?'" [16]

This is a life-changing truth for those who struggle to know God as Father. When we see Jesus, and believe in Him, we too see the Father. Jesus *is* the Father manifest in human flesh.

Jesus is sent by the Father

Those on a mission are sent ones, and Jesus was sent into the world by the Father to fulfil His mission. 'Sent' is the Greek word *apostello,* which means set apart; by implication, Jesus is set apart, sent out on a mission by the Father. [17] What was the mission that Jesus carried? Jesus refers to being 'sent'. He came not to seek His own will but the will of the Father who *sent* Him. Many times in John's Gospel Jesus talks about being 'sent'. He simply says "As the living Father sent Me, and I live because of the Father, so he who feeds on Me will live because of Me." [18]

Jesus tells us that He was sent to 'declare' the Father, or 'reveal' the Father. Jesus, who is God's Son is the only One who could show us or reveal the Father to us, because He and His

---

16 John 14:8-10
17 Strong's from (575) and (47240 'Apostello',set apart, to send out properly on a mission. Literal John 6:57
18 John 6:57

Father are one, and He was at His Father's side or in the bosom of His Father in creation. He was with the Father before the world began. John the disciple says, "No one has seen God at any time. The only begotten Son, who is in the bosom of the Father, He has declared Him." Jesus then answers the Jews who were complaining about Him, referring to Himself, "Not that anyone has seen the Father, except He [Jesus] who is from God; He [Jesus] has seen the Father" (brackets mine). [19]

You must be born again

Nicodemus was a ruler of the Jews who came to Jesus by night because he wanted to ask Jesus about religious matters, just as we do today, without being seen by others. Jesus spoke a profound truth to him:

> "Unless one is born again, he cannot see the kingdom of God … That which is born of the flesh is flesh, and that which is born of the Spirit is spirit. Do not marvel that I say to you, 'You must be born again' … For God so loved the world that He gave His only begotten Son, that whoever believes in Him should not perish but have everlasting life." [20]

Being born into a Christian family didn't mean that I was a Christian. I was taught a lot of theology about the Father, Son and Holy Spirit but what I learnt in my mind didn't change me. I could agree with the principles of truth, but the only way for

---

19 John 1:18; 6:46
20 John 3:5-7,16

me to become a true Christian was to be open to receiving the love of Christ in my heart and to experience a spiritual birth, or to be 'born again' as Jesus told Nicodemus. Revelation of truth isn't learned by the mind, but it comes directly to our heart and spirit as we receive truth from God's Spirit. This is a spiritual birth; God's Spirit giving birth or breathing life into our spirit. As we are 'born again', we receive God's Holy Spirit, and are affirmed as adopted sons and daughters. Now I know that I am adopted into God's family and I am his daughter. Instead of only knowing with my mind, as I'd been taught, I now know in my heart that I am a child of God.

Jesus is the way to the heart of the Father, a place of intimacy, safety and belonging. The relationship is symbolized by a homecoming. Jesus came to tell us the truth about His Father's house, where there are many rooms prepared for each one of us. Jesus is going to prepare a place for each one who believes, and He is coming again to receive you that you may be with him in His Father's house forever. Jesus says, "In My Father's house are many mansions … I go to prepare a place for you." [21] This place of belonging isn't just a promise for the future: it is a present reality for all who believe in Jesus Christ. We are coming home to the Father. He is saying to us, "If anyone loves Me [Jesus] … My Father will love him, and We will come to him and make Our home with him." (brackets mine). [22]

---

21 John 14:2
22 John 14:23

Unity between Father and Son

Unity between Father and Son is as 'One' and He invites us to join Him in this unity, "I in them, and You [Father] in Me" (brackets mine). [23] Jesus makes clear His 'oneness' with His Father by telling his disciples that He could do nothing by Himself:

"The Son can do nothing of Himself, but what He sees the Father do; for whatever He does, the Son also does in like manner … I do not seek My own will but the will of the Father who sent Me … I have not spoken on My own authority; but the Father who sent Me gave Me a command, what I should say and what I should speak … Therefore, whatever I speak, just as the Father has told Me, so I speak". [24]

Jesus reveals the Father

In one of Jesus' final prayers to His Father recorded in John's Gospel Jesus says, "I have finished the work which You have given Me to do." [25] The question that we must ask ourselves is: What is the work that Jesus was given to do? We already know that Jesus shows us the *way* to the Father, but there is more. Jesus' prayer to the Father reveals the truth of his mission. Jesus came to *reveal the Father's name.* This is what He came to do; this is the ultimate reason for Jesus' coming into the world as a babe and living here as a man:

_____

23 John 17:22,23
24 John 5:19,30;12:49,50
25 John 17:4

"I have manifested Your name [Father] to the men whom You have given Me out of the world … O righteous Father! The world has not known You, but I have known You; and these have known that You sent Me. And I have declared to them Your name, and will declare it, that the love with which you loved Me may be in them, and I in them" (brackets mine). [26]

Throughout John's Gospel, Jesus reveals to us His true identity as Son to His Father. Jesus *is* God the Father in human form, so to know Jesus is to know God the Father. To 'make manifest' means to reveal one's true authority and identity. So Jesus made manifest in His human flesh the authority and character of God the Father. To fully know and receive by experience the love of Abba Father only comes as Jesus reveals the Father to us. Jesus ends His prayer to the Father in John 17 by summarizing the completion of His mission. These words of Jesus speak of 'manifesting' and 'revealing' the Father's name to his disciples and continuing to reveal His true identity to all who would believe. So Jesus is unveiling or uncovering the character of His Father and drawing back the curtain of His Father's love.

Jesus reveals the Father to little children

The disciple Matthew tells us that the revelation of the Father doesn't come to the 'wise and prudent' but to 'babes' or innocent ones. Those who have the heart of a child are the

---

26   John 17:6,25,26

ones on whom God looks and reveals His love. "You [Father] have hidden these things from the wise and prudent and have revealed them to babes." Only the Father knows the Son and no one truly knows the Father except the Son and "the one to whom the Son wills [*or chooses*] to reveal Him" (brackets mine). [27]

God says to us, become like little children, and humble yourself in order to receive Jesus. The door to His kingdom is through humility, a bowing low and acknowledging Jesus as Lord. There is no other way to receive Him. Since the beginning of time, man has chosen to go it alone, following the path of pride and self-importance. The way of Jesus is different. He is an upside-down God. The first will be last and the last first. Listen to His voice and come with the heart of a child. Little children have a profound awareness of God.

On November 5th, a young child was taken to a bonfire night celebration with her mum. There was a huge fire and her mother said to her, "Look at that big fire. God says His love is as powerful as a big fire." The child said, "Wow, does everyone in the world know that?" Those with the heart of a child understand the Father's love.

The Father's love

To those of us who have known the love of a good earthly father as well as those who have never received fatherly love, God *is* our loving Father, He *is* our true Dad. Jesus is restoring

---

27 Matthew 11:25-27

relationships and bringing healing to those who haven't been fathered, breathing life into areas in our lives that have shut down. He is redeeming us from the loss, abandonment, rejection and loss of intimacy with Himself and healing of relationship with our earthly dads. This was His mission. As we come to know our heavenly Father, so He makes a way for us to come back into relationship with our natural fathers. This fulfils the prophecy of Malachi that we read about, speaking of the mission of John the Baptist who prepared the way for the coming Messiah, Jesus Christ. "He will turn the hearts of the fathers to the children, and the hearts of the children to their fathers." [28]

The Father is looking for those whose hearts are ready to receive, in whom He can deposit His love. Just as a child opens his heart to a good, earthly dad in complete vulnerability and trust, so the Father is looking for a desperateness in our deep innermost being, a place to deposit His love. In a prayer to the Ephesians, Paul prays "that God the Father, may give to you the spirit of wisdom and revelation in the knowledge of Him, the eyes of your understanding being enlightened". [29]

When our spiritual eyes are opened to God's Spirit, we see like a child. The curtain of our heart is pulled back and we are able to embrace the Father's love. As Jesus was 'sent' into the world, so we too are 'sent' ones, taking the message of the Father's love to the broken and lost, to those who have an orphaned heart. "As the Father has sent Me, I also send you." [30]

---

28 Malachi 4:6
29 Ephesians 1:17,18
30 John 20:21

9 No longer an orphan

"God sent forth His Son, born of a woman, that we might receive the adoption as sons." (Galatians 4:4,5)

Let's go back to the Garden of Eden where the Lord spoke to Adam, as a Father speaks to His son. It was the perfect father/son relationship as God always intended. Adam and Eve were the pinnacle of the Father's creation and they wandered together in the garden enjoying its beauty, talking with God and delighting in each other's presence in the cool of the day. They were in close relationship – a Father with His children – this was true sonship. And this is the beginning of pure emotion, as God intended. Sons and daughters expressing joy, delight, even excitement in their Father's presence.

Ever since the deception in the Garden of Eden, and throughout history, man has continued to eat from the tree of the knowledge of good and evil, searching for true identity and security and trying to find a way to God, but in the wrong way. Adam and Eve were striving to be like God, but a wall of separation came between them and their creator God. The consequences of listening to Satan always leads to a striving to do what is right and trying to find God from a place of pride or self-importance. Those with an orphan heart believe the lie that religious endeavour or religion based on good works is the way to find God and true happiness, but this is a deception. They will never find the unconditional love that they are looking for. Many people who have been deprived of love and recognition are homeless and don't know who their true father is; therefore, they don't have a name, nor is there a sense of history or belonging. Orphans have no inheritance, so fight for what they can get by trying to earn significance through hard work. This search for identity can end up in perfectionism, constantly striving to earn recognition and to prove oneself to a father or to please an authority figure like a boss. No matter how hard you try and how much you allow your success to define who you are, it is impossible to earn credibility or to be noticed by those you are trying to please. The more that achievement isn't recognized, the harder you work to get the attention of those you are trying to impress. It's a vicious circle that doesn't get you anywhere as the bar is always being raised and you will never be good enough.

I know a beautiful lady whose parents had high expectations for her future. Academic achievement was very important for all the children in this family, and seemed to be the only way for them to get their dad's attention. But it was the wrong way, as true love isn't conditional. As a young girl, this lady's fear of failure was so great that she sat her exam for entry to secondary school without writing anything, choosing to fail her exam rather than risk success. She was too frightened to write. Her broken heart was searching for lost identity and security so it was safer to 'fail' the exams, but by doing so she lost her father's love and affirmation.

The story doesn't end there! When my friend married

and had her own young family, she began to question for the first time the lies that she had believed all her life and why she had been taken out of school because of failure. With a huge amount of courage, she decided to risk failure once again by secretly studying for an A level exam just to prove to herself that she wasn't stupid and that there was nothing to be ashamed of. She no longer wanted to be defined by the past, so with much determination, she achieved the goal by getting an 'A' grade in this exam. This was a life-changing experience for my friend and, with God's help, she was able to forgive those who had harmed her and also forgive herself for believing untruths that had controlled her life for so many years. Her negative self-image slowly began to change as she chose to embrace God's truth, that she was wonderfully made in God's image, and had God-given abilities that were waiting to be nurtured and developed.

The truth is that love-starved orphans live with an emptiness on the inside with no deep sense of security. These lost ones are suffering from emotional anorexia. Fathers and mothers have abandoned their children for different reasons, and children also have rejected parents, no longer living as the son or daughter that God originally intended. The orphan spirit affects all human relationships, most significantly family relationships and marriage.

We read in the Old Testament Malachi's prophecy of the hope to come for relationships within families between fathers and children. This is just as relevant today as when it was written. Malachi prophesies of a 'turning' of the hearts of fathers towards the children.[1] This prophecy was fulfilled when Jesus came to save us from the orphan spirit and restore sonship and relationship with God as Father. Jesus is mending the lost and broken in our orphaned world. His mission is to restore fatherhood, so that sons and daughters can rest in the security of being loved unconditionally with nothing to prove. We don't need to earn His approval, but are secure in our God-given identity and are healed as we come to Abba Father through His Son .

George Muller was a 19th century man of God, who was honoured with love and affection in the same way that the Israelites regarded their own prophets. He understood Malachi's prophecy and the need for fathers to turn to the children.

Muller lived in Bristol and built orphan houses for thousands of children who had neither father or mother. In 1865 George Muller wrote a letter to a certain gentleman, inviting him to become the schoolmaster for these orphans. Muller writes, "Your duties are not like those of a teacher in the day school, but more like that of a father, who is at the same time a teacher of his children, as these orphans have no parents and are always under our care. It brings along with it many more enjoyments than those of a teacher in a mere day school; it involves also work and responsibility at certain times when an ordinary day

---

1   Malachi 4:6

teacher has none." [2] Muller understood that the orphans in his care needed fathering as well as instructing. They needed a human father who would reflect the Father heart of God.

It is possible to have good parents and still operate from an orphan heart, trying to earn favour with God through religious endeavour and good works. We will always fail to reach what we are striving for. The only way to know God as Father is through receiving His unconditional love for us, a free gift of God's grace. "For by grace you have been saved through faith, and that not of yourselves; it is the gift of God, not of works, lest anyone should boast." [3]

Just like some of us, some of Jesus' disciples had good earthly fathers, [4] yet Jesus still called them orphans, "I will not leave you orphans." [5] Jesus recognizes spiritual poverty, and promises never to leave us as orphans. In the context of this verse, Jesus was speaking to the disciples about His death and resurrection to come, and recognized that the disciples didn't want Him to leave them when He ascended to His Father. Jesus then reassures them of the Father's promise to send the gift of the Holy Spirit who would remain with them for ever. "I will pray the Father, and He will give you another Helper, that He may abide with you forever – the Spirit of truth." [6] And as we receive God's Spirit into our hearts, He is forever with us.

---

2   W.M. Capper & D Johnson, A R Short. 1954, Intervarsity Fellowship, London WC1, p97,98

3   Ephesians 2:8,9

4   Matthew 4:18-21

5   John 14:18

6   John 14:16

We truly become God's spiritual sons and daughters when we receive the gift of the Holy Spirit. The Father sends the Spirit of His Son into our heart, so that we are adopted as sons and daughters into the family of God. "God sent forth His Son…that we might receive the adoption as sons … because you are sons, God has sent forth the Spirit of His Son into your hearts, crying out, 'Abba Father!'" [7]

In this verse 'adoption' is the Greek word *huiothesia* meaning sonship given to 'one to whom it does not naturally belong' distinct from a relationship consequent upon birth. [8] So believers are given the spirit of sonship and adopted into the family of God, as sons and daughters. The Holy Spirit is sent to believers from the Father who witnesses with our spirit that we are adopted into His family.

There are only three places in the New Testament where the Aramaic term 'Abba' is used, referring to God as Father. Mark's Gospel describes the scene in the Garden of Gethsemane, where Jesus addresses His Father in the most intimate way, at one of His deepest moments, calling out to 'Abba' to take the cup of suffering from Him as He becomes the object of the Father's wrath. [9] Jesus speaks to His Father as 'Abba', just as a child would express complete trust in a father.

The word 'Abba' is used as an invitation to those who have received the spirit of adoption. We now share the family

7   Galatians 4:4-6
8   W.E Vine, Vine's Expository Dictionary of Old and New Testament Words. 1997, Thomas Nelson, Nashville, Tennessee
9   Mark 14:36

name and can say 'Abba, Father'. We have the same intimate relationship with the Father that Jesus had when we receive the Spirit of adoption and call Him 'Abba':

"For as many as are led by the Spirit of God, these are sons of God. For you did not receive the spirit of bondage again to fear, but you received the Spirit of adoption by whom we cry out, 'Abba Father.' The Spirit Himself bears witness with our spirit that we are children of God, and if children, then heirs – heirs of God." [10]

Some children are adopted at birth. One of my very first jobs was working in a home for single parents. The teenage mothers, some as young as fourteen, had to leave their home community and travel many miles away to the city, because there was such a stigma attached to their illegitimate pregnancy. When the young mum came into labour, she was taken to a hospital to give birth. As she did so, a screen was put between the mother and baby, so that the mum didn't see the baby, she only heard the cry! The babies were taken away for adoption and the mother then returned to her own family as if nothing had happened. It was such a traumatic experience for these teenagers.

When a child is adopted, just like these orphaned, unwanted babies, they are chosen and, in the eyes of the law, they now belong to the adoptive parents. By law, sonship is given to whom it doesn't naturally belong. In the same way, our Father chooses to adopt us into His family, even though we don't deserve His love and grace. Ephesians too refers to *huiothesia*:

---

10 Romans 8:14-17

"He chose us in Him before the foundation of the world … having predestined us to adoption as sons by Jesus Christ." [11]

God wanted us as His sons and daughters. As believers we receive the Spirit of adoption, that is, the Holy Spirit produces in us the realization of sonship, adoption as sons. It's through the Holy Spirit that the Father's DNA bears witness with our spirits that we are children of God. The Holy Spirit is the confirmation of our adoption. The work of God's Spirit is to bring us out of orphan-ness and back into sonship. As the human spirit unites with the Spirit of the Father, we become sons and daughters, no longer orphans.

Through adoption, we are set free and delivered from the slavery and spirit of fear experienced by all orphans, which began in the Garden of Eden. In both Romans and Galatians, Paul says that because we are now sons, we are free: "no longer a slave, but a son". [12] This is the liberating experience for all who believe. When I prayed to receive God's Spirit, I had no expectations of what might happen. But immediately I knew that I was a child of God. It truly was liberating! For the first time I had no doubt that I was born again, and knew at last what it meant to be a Christian.

Receiving the Holy Spirit affirms our identity as adopted sons and daughters of the Father of all fathers. A spiritual transaction takes place as "the love of God has been poured

---

11   Ephesians 1:4,5
12   Romans 8:15; Galatians 4:7

out into our hearts through the Holy Spirit who was given to us". [13] As adopted children, we are now heirs of God and joint heirs with Christ enjoying all the privileges and inheritance rights of God's children. The Spirit Himself bears witness with our spirit that we are children of God and, if children, then heirs – heirs of God.

Our response to the revelation of the Father's love is to humble ourselves and receive, kneeling before the Father who names all families on earth. Whatever our experience of family and fathering, God's children can approach the Father with boldness, acknowledging that He is the source of fatherhood and 'Father' is God's family name.

As we pray to God, He says, "You are now my son, my daughter, and I am your Father. You have come to me willingly, under no compulsion. You are not trapped; I will not harm you. I AM love. The source of all love is from Me. Just as a good earthly father carries their child, so I bend down, and pick you up when you fall over. You don't need to keep your distance anymore; I have drawn back the curtain, and I welcome you into My house. This is why I sent My Son, to show you who I am. I am your Father."

---

13 Romans 5:5

10 The love of a father

Jesus tells us a parable (an earthly story with a heavenly meaning) in Luke's Gospel chapter 15 illustrating the relationships in a family between a loving father and his sons. The father had two sons, born into a privileged home. The brothers had all the advantages of sonship, including the promise of an inheritance. The younger son demanded his inheritance before his father's death, and set off from his father's house, wasting his father's money, and all his inheritance on reckless living. The word 'prodigal' means 'recklessly wasteful' or 'extravagant'. As time went on he ran out of money and there was a famine in the land.

The 'prodigal' son came to his senses and realized that the servants in his father's house had more than he had; they had food to eat and enough left over. He felt guilty and condemned about what he'd done and, overcome with shame he humbled himself, and returned to his father. The only way home was to admit his error, say sorry and ask for forgiveness from his dad.

His identity was shattered. He felt more like a servant or an orphan than a son. It is possible to live as an orphan even though born a son.

The father, seeing him in the distance, extravagantly loved his son, and came running towards him, embracing him. A true father never rejects his sons. We see the love of a father as he lavishes undeserved 'reckless or wasteful' love on the son who had rejected him and wasted his inheritance. The father then calls the true servants, "Bring out the best robe and put it on him, and put a ring on his hand and sandals on his feet." [1] These items are the signs of true sonship.

But there were two orphan sons in this story. The older brother had lived in his father's house all his life, serving religiously and never disobeying his father's commands at any time. The dutiful older son was jealous and complained. This angry son didn't refer to his father as 'father' nor did he acknowledge his brother when he returned. He didn't have the heart of a son towards his father, but he was selfish, justifying himself, to please and gain acceptance with his father by working hard and obeying all the rules. He too had an orphan's heart rather than the heart of a son. In other words, his religious pride was the basis of his relationship with his father. All along he remained in his father's house, but his heart was orphaned. Orphans serve in order to prove their identity and acceptance, but sons and daughters know their true identity and serve from a position of humility and security in the Father's love.

Jesus speaks about our identity as sons and daughters. Our identity isn't determined by our good works. Our God-given unshakeable identity was secured for us when Jesus defeated death, sin and Satan on our behalf and invited us to join Him in union with His Father. When we return to the Father, there is a homecoming, just as it was with the 'prodigal son'. We find that our identity is in union with the Father. He loves us in the same way that He loves Jesus.

---

1   Luke 15:22

The same love with which Abba Father loves Jesus is the same love with which He loves all those who are returning home to the Father. Just as the prodigal son turned his life around and ran home to his father, so the Father welcomes home many orphaned sons and daughters today whose hearts are broken and those who are tired of obeying all the religious rules. He loves the lost, the anxious, the disappointed, the traumatized. What an amazing invitation, for us to come home and to dwell with the Father in His house. We are no longer homeless or abandoned. The Father is restoring our orphan hearts, and providing a safe place for us in His house. There's plenty of room and every person matters. When we recognize that we too have an orphaned heart, our heavenly Dad sees us and has compassion: He runs and comes close to kiss.

God promises to make a home for the orphan, because the Father loves them: "We [Father and Son] will come to him [orphans] and make Our home with him" [2] (brackets mine). He says, "I am your Father."

We mustn't miss this opportunity to receive Jesus' welcome just like the lost son. Jesus brings life to the world and is restoring and recovering the lost. God is a loving Father who welcomes home the prodigals, the poor, the homeless and the vulnerable. His house is full of prodigals, and He has many rooms, and is preparing a place for more. His children are secure forever. Just as Jesus was sent into the world on a mission, so He sends us into the world with the same message

---

2   John 14:23

of the Father's love to the prodigals. Prodigals are coming home.

The following prayer is for those who have run away from God and are returning to the Father, and being welcomed into His house:

"Father, may my identity never be defined by what I do or don't do. May the revelation of the Father's love give me the courage to simply be who God created me to be. May I carry within my being the knowledge that I am a much-loved child of the Father. May my identity as a son or daughter be enough even in the midst of a world, and sometimes a church, that demands more from me."

Part Five:
REDEMPTION

11 Earthly fathers

"I bow my knees to the Father of our Lord Jesus Christ, from whom the whole family in heaven and earth is named." *(Ephesians 3:14)*

In families, parents give names to children, so their unique identity is linked to the parents by their name. This verse in Ephesians 3 tells us that the God of the Bible is the creator of all things, so the whole family in heaven and on earth is named by the Father through whom comes our spiritual identity linked to His name, Father. We have to remember that we are all made in the image of Creator Father, but we become true children of God when we believe in Him, "as many as received Him [Jesus], He gave the right to become children of God, to those who believe in His name" (brackets mine). [1]

Our earthly dad is the one person who should always be there for us, the one we turn to when we need advice about making difficult decisions, or just comfort when we feel lonely. Many people have had the privilege of a secure, stable relationship with their father who was there when they needed him, in a loving home environment. The family is a place of security. For others, family has become a place of fear, a place of abuse – emotional, physical or sexual. A normal, loving parental relationship with the people we call 'Mum' or 'Dad' has broken down.

---

1   John 1:12

God our Father is our heavenly Dad who is constant, and trustworthy and promises never to reject us or leave us as an orphan. He is the Father of the fatherless. The Bible says, "Even if my father and mother abandon me, the LORD will hold me close." [2] So my response is, "I bow my knees to the Father of our Lord Jesus Christ, from whom the whole family in heaven and earth is named." [3]

Right from the beginning we see that all earthly dads are made in the image of God the Father, a shadow or a reflection of true fatherhood. A healthy father gives us his time and attention, so we are nurtured and feel loved, able to reach our true potential in life. We all need a dad to protect us and help us to flourish physically and spiritually as we are physical and spiritual beings. The emotional gap on the inside is filled by our dad or father substitute who will symbolize God to us.

Good fathers

We have all been fathered, whether from our biological dad or from another father figure as part of a blended family. Children need to be loved and nurtured. We might have happy memories of warmth, laughter, fun and being cared for by loving parents who drew the best out of us so that we would became secure in our identity, the person God intended us to be. Home was a healthy and secure place where the needs of childhood were met. This is such a blessing, and fathers are to

---

2   Psalm 27:10 NLT
3   Ephesians 3:14-21

be honoured. The Bible talks about our response to parents; that is, being a true son or daughter to our earthly father.

In the Old Testament Moses teaches fathers how they should instruct and model their faith to their children which is just as relevant today as in the day the words were written:

" Love the Lord your God and serve Him with all your heart and soul … commit yourselves wholeheartedly to these words of mine. Teach them to your children. Talk about them when you are at home and when you are on the road, when you are going to bed and when you are getting up. Write them on the doorposts of your house and on your gates." [4]

The New Testament also helps us understand how to parent and repeats the Old Testament command to honour your father and mother, with the promise that if we do, "it may go well with you and that you may enjoy long life on the earth". [5] God is reminding us to honour parents and esteem them highly. Honouring can be described as esteeming highly, showing respect. This is the first commandment with God's promise of blessing and fruitfulness. There are times when we fail to give honour where it is due, but, as we say sorry, Jesus forgives us for not truly honouring our parents.

Choosing to forgive is the key to good relationships within family life, and we need to stay in forgiveness and unity, and "to bear with one another in love". [6] And remembering too that

---

4   Deuteronomy 11:13-22 NLT
5   Ephesians 6:1,2
6   Colossians 3:13, Ephesians 4:2

"love covers a multitude of sins". [7] Broken fathers reproduce brokenness, but a good father trains and instructs his children in love and doesn't 'exasperate' them or crush their spirits which can end up in rebellion. [8]

Absent fathers

We expect our family to be secure but sometimes in our communities the opposite is true. The family can be a lonely place because of emotional or physical neglect at the heart of it. Dads can be physically and emotionally absent for many reasons, sometimes ending in marriage breakdown and divorce, resulting in single parent families. Many children for whatever reason don't know who their father is, so physical contact with a dad is missing, leaving a huge emotional gap in their lives. In addition, dads can be so preoccupied with working long hours that unintentional physical absence becomes a way of life. Long hours at work, commuting and pressure to provide an income can be an excuse for absence from the home, so children don't feel valued because dad is too busy.

Another pattern is the dad who lives at home but is emotionally absent and passive. It is possible for children to be orphaned by an emotionally absent dad who is physically present but out of touch with his own feelings, and so unable to express love to his own children. This dad loves with his head and not his heart, thinking that he is showing love by

---

7   Proverbs 10:12
8   Ephesians 6:4

working hard in the office to provide for the family. The pain of abandonment is passed down through the generations so hurting dads hurt their children. Fathers who have never known a true father's love in their own lives and have experienced personal rejection from their own dad are often unable to fully love their children.

When dads or mums are absent physically or emotionally, children feel let down and ignored and there will be a part of the child that is missing emotionally because he or she wasn't called into life by dad. It is possible to be emotionally starved without even realizing it, because the child hasn't known anything else. Love deprivation has become the norm and a way of life. The phrase "children should be seen and not heard" is the opposite of what Jesus taught. He said, "Let the children come to Me, and do not forbid them." [9] Every child is special, and their emotions are crying out to be nurtured by the people they call 'Mum' or 'Dad'.

It has been documented that children brought up in orphanages suffer from emotional neglect and social isolation, which manifests in depression, anxiety and feelings of sadness. They are unable to deal with the grief and sense of loss because they haven't had the physical and emotional contact with a mother or father. [10] Even adopted children who are re-named by well-meaning adopting parents can struggle to have a sense of identity and worth, a deep emotional loss.

---

9   Matthew 19:14

10   www.hopeandhomes.org

The trauma of being abandoned by an earthly dad means that children don't want to know God as Father at all because the pain is too deep. Their view of God is distorted and limited, so they push God away. An absent dad represents a distant God.

Abusive fathers or mothers

Abuse from a dad or responsible adult may be emotional, verbal, physical or even sexual, which is deeply harmful to a child, causing breakdown in trust and rejection of the father figure and ultimately God. Children on the receiving end of all forms of abuse find it difficult to maintain healthy relationships and withdraw into themselves as a form of self-protection and a way of avoiding further conflict. There is a tendency to self-blame or even self-harm.

Sadly, many children have an abusive or absent father, like the daughter of a friend of mine. My friend's partner became physically abusive and as a consequence was arrested and served a prison sentence. Their daughter lived with me for several weeks while her mother recovered in hospital. The only hope for broken families is to point them to their perfect Dad, who is father to the fatherless, defends the widows, and will never abandon them. He is the Father that our earthly dad could never be, and will never leave us nor forsake us.

If our earthly father was absent or abusive, there will be a void and emotional emptiness on the inside. Acknowledging the inner void brought about by the absence of an earthly father's love is the beginning of healing, which takes time. The person we call 'dad' might be physically or emotionally absent or he has become an unknown father figure who is just a name but not a person. The thought of knowing Abba Father personally and intimately is meaningless or even undesirable; consequently we can be repelled by the thought of 'father', let alone wanting emotional warmth and longing for closeness.

Kate suffered emotional and verbal abuse from a parent, and consequently was trapped in a cycle of anorexia. Even though she felt hungry and was desperate to eat, she would walk past food, unable to allow herself to eat. The less she ate, the less she wanted to eat. It took years for the cycle to be broken. Escaping into a lifestyle of anorexia was the only way for this young lady to take control of her own life. My friend was left to find her own answers to life, which she did eventually by forgiving her mother, and trusting that God was her perfect Dad who would never abuse her. She hid in His shelter and heard the words of her heavenly Father saying to her "I'm proud of you."

Sexual abuse is common, often hidden and not spoken about even in adult life. I met a young girl who on one occasion was assaulted by an older man who pinned her against a wall, and started kissing her. The trauma caused her to lose her voice for some while, but because she was able to escape and run away from the man, she didn't talk about this for years, thinking it wasn't important. Abuse causes us to hide because of the secrecy and feelings hopelessness, shame and trauma.

No matter what happens, and however insignificant abuse feels, we need never be afraid to get help and talk about it as the way to begin the process of inner healing.

We have to remind ourselves not to allow our past to determine our future. The last thing we want is to be robbed of the present because of past experiences. By forgiving the abuser you will be released from the memory of trauma and then God as Father who sees all the hidden secrets of the heart will reach deep inside to heal and bring wholeness. Any form of abuse is not what God intended, and the victim is not to blame.

Authoritarian father

For some, God is a distant Father, an authoritarian figure like a policeman in the sky who is unapproachable and One who people believe punishes those who don't keep all the religious rules. When things go wrong, or we don't feel good enough, we are frightened of this distant, angry God. This view of God is often taught, or modelled by a strict, earthly dad or authority figure rather than by a nurturing, loving and forgiving father. Authoritarian fathers can have unreasonable expectations for their children with achievement being the only way to try and earn his acceptance. The bar is set very high.

I know a young man who desperately wanted affirmation from his strict father. His father had high expectations for him, so he decided to study law at university. This young man thought that by academic achievement he would at last win his father's attention and approval so when he eventually finished the course he invited his father to the degree show. But his dad didn't go or appear to be interested. Rather than congratulating his son, his only comment was, "You could have tried harder."

My friend was desperately trying to earn his father's love and affection through achievement, but it was the wrong way round. Love can't be earned, no matter how hard we try. This young man realized that he couldn't earn his father's love. Instead he let go of bitterness, and chose to forgive his dad who himself suffered from past failures. Forgiveness unlocked the man's heart, so that he was able to approach God without fear of punishment. He found that, as he did so, his heart became soft, and he knew a closer intimacy with his heavenly Dad. This was a new relationship that he wasn't familiar with especially because he hadn't known perfect love from his own birth dad. God isn't a distant, judgmental, critical and angry Father but close to us all the time as it says in the Bible, "He is not far from each one of us; for in Him we live and move and have our being." [11] The trauma of an authoritarian father figure brings pain to the heart of God, who is the perfect Dad – a good, good Father, the One who is there to give comfort and nurture. He is our provider, our ever-present Dad who is more than any earthly dad could ever be for us. The truth is that Abba Father says that He will not leave us as orphans, whatever our story or experiences of an earthly dad. The

---

11   Acts 17:27,28

revelation of knowing God as Father brings healing and hope to broken lives as we find it in our hearts to forgive those who have harmed us.

My friend John was diagnosed with leukaemia. He struggled to forgive his mother who judged him for not following the religious customs that he had been taught. After a long process of turmoil this man was able to admit that by not forgiving his mother, he was punishing himself and growing bitter. The only way to be set free and become secure in his own identity was through forgiveness. Luke's Gospel tells us of how Jesus forgave a paralysed man of all his sins, and also healed him of his sickness. [12] Just as the paralysed man came to Jesus, many years ago, so my friend John came to Jesus, the One who forgives all sin. He confessed and admitted his bitter attitude towards his mother and was able to forgive her. As he did this, he was completely healed of his leukaemia. This was life changing for John as he recovered and received into his life the true love of the Father.

Emotional healing from abuse and abandonment is a gradual process of recovery but it is possible to be free and made whole after long-term loss and disappointment. It does take time to build trust in people and in God. Our hearts need to be nurtured just like a child and come to life maybe for the first time. Recovery happens as we listen to the words of Jesus and take Him at His word, then past memories of emotional loss and torment are removed and we will be liberated to be

---

12   Luke 5:17-39

the person God originally made and intended us to be.

God is our Father and, as we grow in trust, He begins the process of restoring all that has been lost. He brings hope and healing from damaged emotions, filling the vacuum; it's never too late to get help. God's Spirit reaches right back to early childhood, touching secret areas and scars and supernaturally healing deep pain, past and present. Through His death on the cross, He takes away the sting from trauma and restores our emotional damage. As you trust your heavenly Dad, you will leave behind your broken identity and move to a place of safety and emotional security.

However intentional your father was, he still fell short: he never could fully be the father that God had in mind. God never intended for parents to abuse or abandon their children, leaving them with foster carers or in orphanages. This wasn't the plan of the Father from the beginning. He never designed children to be torn apart by the loss of a father. Knowing God as a good Father is the way forwards, the way to be healed of all past pain. Sometimes we struggle with the idea that God is a 'good' Father, because we define God by what He didn't do; things go wrong in life, and sometimes we have been unfairly treated. But the truth is that God does care and He knows all about our disappointments. As we learn to trust Him, we discover that that He is close by, and He loves us more than an earthly parent could ever love.

Prayers of forgiveness for my earthly dad who was an absent father, either physically or emotionally

Father God, I forgive my father for not being there for me. He left home before I really knew him and hasn't been in touch with me since. I forgive him for being an absent father. Father, I give you my loss and pain, and now receive your love as my true Father.

Father God, I forgive my dad for having been emotionally absent. He didn't know how to express love verbally, nor show physical emotion because of being out of touch with his own emotions. I choose to break the cycle of emotional lack in my family. I choose to love my children with all my emotions and show them love verbally, physically, regularly saying "I love you".

Father God, I forgive my dad for being physically absent because of work demands and business. I forgive him for not understanding that I needed to be nurtured, and wanted him emotionally and physically, more than he realized, in Jesus' name.

Prayers of forgiveness for those who abused me verbally, physically or sexually

Father I forgive my parents for their anger and verbal abuse, beyond what was appropriate for a child to experience. I receive your love for me; heavenly Father you are my perfect dad.

Father, I forgive men who acted towards me in an inappropriate manner and caused untold emotional damage. I loose myself from all memories of past abuse and walk free from the pain and trauma in Jesus' name.

I forgive my father or mother who abused me physically as a result of alcoholism, using force beyond what was appropriate for a grown adult. I forgive my parents for allowing me to witness my father being physically abusive towards other family members which frightened me. I am set free from the memories and pain of all physical abuse in Jesus' name.

Prayer of forgiveness for authoritarian parents

God my Father, I forgive my earthly father and mother for being too strict and impatient and not understanding me. I'm sorry too for rejecting you God as my heavenly Father because I thought you were like my dad. Father, thank you that you love me, and accept me as I am.

12 Mentoring sons and daughters

All of us at some time in our lives will need a mentor to support us emotionally or psychologically especially if we haven't known the love of a natural father or mother. We too will become mentors to others. Mentors are role models, within a loving, secure relationship, who give encouragement and provide a safe place of accountability which might have been missing in our own family. The aim is for each person to grow in faith, as well as in giftings and callings, in order to reach their full potential in life. Our ultimate security is in God our Father, as He affirms our true identity as His sons or daughters.

In our generation, some adult children have chosen to leave families where spiritual abuse has led to rejection by parents or rejection of parents. I know stories of young people who have left strict religious families in order to be free to discover their own pathway to God, or in some cases have rejected the God that they were brought up to believe in. It takes a lot of courage to receive counselling from a mature mentor and to question those who you love, in order to be true to yourself. Remember, the God of the Bible is to be trusted, and , He says to us today, "Do not fear; put your hand into the hand of your Father. I will never reject you nor leave you as an orphan. I am your perfect Father."

"Even if my father and mother abandon me, the Lord will hold me close." [1]

I spent time supporting and encouraging a growing family where sadly the father, who suffered from alcoholism, left his Christian wife and children as he tried to break his addiction through rehabilitation and detox. My friend was keen for me to share her story, in order to help deter others who are trapped in a life of alcohol abuse. Not only has my friend lost a husband, but also her children have lost their dad. My friend needs Christian friends who will believe in her and stand alongside her, encouraging her as she mothers her children and fills the gap left by an absent father. She says with faith, "God is using many people to call the father of my children back. I know God wants to save him."

For those who have lost their own earthly father, as spiritual fathers and mothers we can show them their perfect Dad, who won't abandon them. He is the Father that our earthly dad could never be, who will never leave us nor forsake us. In the Bible, we read that God has compassion on His children; He is tender and compassionate to those who fear Him.

Paul

The apostle Paul shows us how to be a mentor. He wasn't only a teacher and leader but talks about himself as a spiritual father and as a mother comforting her newborn, "… we were gentle among you, just as a nursing mother cherishes her own

---

1   Psalm 27:10 NLT

children." And then as a father, "we exhorted and comforted, and charged every one of you, as a father does his own children, that you would walk worthy of God." [2]

Paul was involved in the spiritual journey of the people he mentored. He 'gave birth' spiritually to new believers in Christ: "… you might have ten thousand instructors in Christ, yet you do not have many fathers; for in Christ Jesus I have begotten you through the gospel." [3]

Paul also tells us about the young believers who he fathered and mentored. "I have sent Timothy to you, who is my beloved and faithful son in the Lord." [4] Paul talks of 'birthing' and 'labouring', until Christ is formed in the lives of young Christians, particularly Timothy. His relationship with young believers is so relevant to us today. He talks of those he mentors as "My little children, for whom I labour in birth again until Christ is formed in you." [5] Just as a mother gives birth to her children, so Paul acted as a spiritual midwife, birthing sons and daughters through the gospel.

Timothy

We imitate the lifestyle of spiritual fathers and mothers probably more than their words. Paul loved his spiritual children, Timothy and Titus, and he honoured them. Timothy was the son of a Jewish woman, 'who believed' and a Greek

2   1 Thessalonians 2:7,11
3   1 Corinthians 4:15
4   1 Corinthians 4:17
5   Galatians 4:19

father, but was the spiritual son of Paul, "you know his [Timothy's] proven worth, how as a son with his father [Paul] he served with me in the gospel" (brackets mine). [6]

We can learn a lot from Paul's relationship to Timothy and his role as a father. He talks about Timothy "as a true son in the faith" and he encourages Timothy, his beloved son, "to be strong in the grace that is in Christ Jesus". Paul as his father in the Lord reminds his spiritual son Timothy not to neglect the spiritual gifts that are in him but exhorts him to "stir up the gift of God which is in you through the laying on of my hands". [7] In the same way, we can encourage those who we mentor to grow in their faith and use the gifts that God has given them. Paul urges Timothy to "wage the good warfare" over the prophetic words previously given to him, and he was to mix the prophetic words given him with "faith and a good conscience" in order to see the words fulfilled. [8]

Honour is important, and we see that the mark of a good spiritual parent is to honour and affirm less mature Christians, and speak well of them. Paul constantly encourages and affirms Timothy as a young man, urging others not to despise his youth, and for him to be an example to the believers "in word, in conduct, in love, in spirit, in faith, in purity". [9] Paul tells the church in Corinth to welcome Timothy as his spiritual

---

6   Philippians 2:22
7   2 Timothy 1:6
8   1 Timothy 1:18,19
9   1 Timothy 4:12

son who imitated Paul as his true spiritual father without despising him or causing him to be discouraged.

Titus, Mark, Onesimus

Paul honoured his spiritual son Titus as "a true son in our common faith". [10] Paul cared for Titus, and recommended him to the church of Corinth. Mark is another of Paul's spiritual sons. Paul asks the church to welcome him as "a beloved son". A special son of Paul's was Onesimus, whom Paul says "I have begotten while in my chains". In other words, Paul fulfilled the role of spiritual midwife to his spiritual son Onesimus who was born again while in prison. [11] Paul says, once he was a slave but now he is a "beloved brother, especially to me". [12] Paul's life was an example of a loving spiritual father, honouring where honour is due, and living by example. We can learn so much from Paul who wasn't married, but who fulfilled the role of spiritual father.

John

John, the disciple of Jesus who revealed the true identity of Jesus as the Son of His Father is most qualified to teach us how to father and be a spiritual guide to those in our care. Because of his intimacy with Jesus, John's eyes were opened to revelation of the Father so he was able to father the next generation of believers, carrying in himself the message of

---

10 Titus 1:4
11 Philemon 10
12 Philemon 16

God's love. Just as Jesus was sent into the world, so He sends us into the world with the message of the Father's love. John records the words of Jesus, "As the Father has sent Me, I also send you." [13] Just as He obeyed the command to pass on the revelation of the Father's love to his spiritual 'children', those he fathered, so must we.

John encourages the 'little children', young men and fathers regardless of their age. [14] These are the ones on whom the Father has given His love, those He calls His children, the ones who 'are born of God'. John urges his little children not to sin, that they "abide in Him and not be ashamed at His coming", to "keep yourself from idols" and "let no one deceive you'. [15] John declares over his little children [believers], "You are of God, little children, and have overcome them [the antichrist], because He who is in you is greater than he who is in the world" (brackets mine). [16] John's greatest vision and joy was that his spiritual children continue to walk in the faith. [17]

Over a period of ten years, I was mentoring and encouraging a well-educated friend who had come to live in the UK following her arranged marriage at a young age. At first she was afraid even to speak English, but she gradually became confident and adjusted to life in her adopted country as I helped her with her studies. My friend knew that I was a

---

13 John 20:21
14 1 John 2:12-14
15 1 John 3:1,7; 2:8; 5:21
16 1 John 4:4
17 3 John 4

Christian, and she would often ask me to pray for her. This was a long-distance race alongside my friend until eventually, as a pace setter, I left her to run on her own.

I knew that being a parent and spiritual mentor to my own children was my first priority as a mother. This is a lifelong calling for all mothers and takes time and perseverance. I'd also learnt through experience and watching other families, that secure and well-balanced children don't just happen. I needed to learn to love and invest in my own relationship with Jesus Christ, in order to be in a secure enough place to nurture and demonstrate love to my own children, however inadequately. This was a daily commitment from the beginning. I knew that I was called to watch and pray over my sons and daughter, and eventually their husband and wives and my grandchildren, and by God's grace affirming and speaking truth into their lives.

13 Knowing God as Father

*"There may be so-called gods both in heaven and on earth
… But for us there is one God the Father, by whom all things
were created and for whom we live. And there is one Lord,
Jesus Christ, through whom all things were created and
through whom we live." (1 Corinthians 8:5,6 NLT)*

I befriended a lovely young lady who wanted to know more
about this God I called Father. But for my friend, this was
costly. We chose to meet in secret to talk about the Christian
faith, as my friend was veiled. One day I gave her a New
Testament, which she hid very carefully so that no one would
find this precious gift that came to mean everything to her.
She had many questions, particularly to do with being sure
about eternal life which she hadn't been able to find in her own
religion. In a dream she had a vision of Christian believers
entering a church in her home country and receiving the
Lord's Supper, which she came to understand was symbolic
of the death of Jesus Christ, the Son of God. There came a
day when my friend chose to renounce the faith that she had
grown up with. She was paying a high price as she walked
away from what had become so familiar to her and she still
had many questions about God and even feared to trust the
God of the Bible. When she took off her veil things began
to change dramatically. First of all my friend was forced into
hiding without her children. Then, one day, I received a phone

call from a family member forbidding me to ever speak to my friend again. It was quite a shock and I never found out the end of the story, but pray that she chooses to follow Jesus, the one who promises that whoever believes shall have the gift of eternal life.

We are all on our own spiritual journey, searching for truth, and progress will vary. The important thing is not to give up, as God never gives up on us! He cares about each of us individually. The path to knowing God as Father is ongoing, but as we begin to trust God as Father, the Father above all fathers, our hope will be restored, particularly where there has been deprivation in relationships with our earthly dad.

We might never have been aware of God as Father and His nurturing presence providing deep security. Instead, our security was in the natural human way of thinking, unconsciously responding to the lies about our identity that we had absorbed over the years. Everything that doesn't line up with what God says about our identity is a lie and can now be rejected. As we admit our emotional emptiness, and repent of our unbelief as well as forgive those who have hurt us, the desire to know God as Father will slowly grow on the inside. It's as if a light is turned on in this area of life that has previously been in darkness and orphaned. Discovering the Father's love is a 'spiritual' journey, as we embrace our true identity as sons and daughters in the way that God the Father intended. We begin to believe the truth, and not the lies.

The key to trusting God as Father is to ask His Holy Spirit

to come into our lives. He is the One who convicts us of the truth about Jesus. As we say sorry for our unbelief, His love will fill our heart and spirit, and then our minds begin to process what we are receiving. Knowing the Father can't be taught but it is something that is 'caught' by faith. Truth comes into our heart and mind, and then our emotions and feelings are transformed. God heals our empty souls and inner person, and replaces fear with His love. He isn't to be feared. This is an ongoing journey of faith as Jesus continues to make known the Father's love to us. You can read about it here, "There is no fear in love; but perfect love casts out fear, because fear involves torment." [1] "I have revealed you [Father] to them and I will continue to do so" (brackets mine). [2]

Our journey of faith, of knowing the Father's love, often starts with the realization that we had no desire to know God as Father. It was outside our reality. But as we begin to trust God, and let go of our past religious teaching, we find that it is more important to trust God than to worry about what other people think. Our heavenly Father loves us in the same way that He loves Jesus. Jesus was sent into the world to show us the Father's love. He continues to reveal His love as a gift to us, like gold treasure which when found makes everything else pale into insignificance.

Jesus came into an orphan world to reveal the Father to each of us, and bring restoration of father and son relationships

---

1   1 John 4:18
2   John 17:26

as it was in the beginning in the Garden of Eden. This was His mission, for which He was sent into the world. The truth is that Jesus says, I no longer leave you as orphans and this applies to us today as we are adopted into His family. Prodigals are coming home, back to the Father!

For those who have suffered loss, rejection, abandonment, abuse from a father figure, Jesus is saying that, although we live in a fallen world, we can learn intimacy from our perfect Dad. He can be trusted. We all have imperfect, fallen earthly fathers, who make mistakes and some have suffered from absent fathers. The legacy of broken marriges, divorce, single parents struggling to parent children on their own can be healed. Whatever happens in this life, Jesus came into the world to redeem and to restore our broken lives. Satan entered the world in the beginning to kill, steal and destroy but Jesus comes to bring life, healing and wholeness to the orphan heart.

This message is good news to lost and broken people and particularly the fatherless. Broken people hurt people, broken fathers hurt their children, but Jesus came to lift you out of this cycle of harm. You are no longer an orphan. The journey to receiving the Father's love is an ongoing spiritual, emotional and physical one of healing.

God the Father is the perfect father; one our earthly father could never be. There is the key to receiving the Father's love which unlocks the healing process. By repenting of our own sins and forgiving or even acknowledging that we have difficulty forgiving our earthly dad or the person we call 'dad' is the starting point. Forgiveness is a choice. We choose to forgive our dad or even an authority figure for not truly representing God the Father to us. Many dads suffered themselves as children, so a pattern of hurts and wounds and layers of wounding often causes anger and bitterness to build up in their hearts being passed down through the generations. Choosing to forgive from the heart will be an act of the will not an emotional response to a set of circumstances. Forgiveness is often a process, a choosing to forgive over and over again, seventy times seven as Jesus says, but forgiveness does bear fruit. As we forgive, God the Father is able to begin work in the lives of our abusers, bringing conviction, and pouring in His love as he softens our hearts.

One day I met a beautiful lady on a train as I travelled to London and we started talking. My friend came from Somalia, and during the civil war in the 1980s, her family fled the country as refugees. She was the youngest of six children, and as the family left the country by boat, her mother made the decision to leave her five-year-old child behind, all alone on the quay. The mother thought that her young child would surely be noticed and cared for by a humanitarian charity. This is exactly what happened. She was rescued by Médecins Sans Frontières and eventually found herself in England. Thirty years later here she was having the conversation with me on the train, a story she hadn't forgotten. She knew through the family network that her mother was alive, and desperately wanted to contact her daughter. I asked my friend whether she could ever forgive her mother, and she said, "NO! I will never forgive her, and will never have contact with my mother." I prayed in my heart, asking the Lord for a key to unlock this sad story. Words came to me and I said to my friend, "A mother never forgets her child. Your mother regrets what she did and is truly sorry. She realized that she made a mistake, and it was a wrong decision." I talked about forgiveness, about Jesus forgiving us all our sins, and that by not forgiving, my friend was punishing herself, not her mother. As I spoke to the woman, I could feel her heart softening, and eventually she agreed to contact her mother. She even said that she wanted to forgive her mother.

Forgiveness isn't dependent upon the other person forgiving us, but it's a free choice that liberates us from all injustices that have held us in bondage. Forgiveness is letting go of those who've caused offense and reclaiming our lives back so that we can be the person God intended. If we don't forgive, we are the one who suffers, not our abusers. Jesus talks about forgiveness, "If you forgive those who sin against you, your heavenly Father will forgive you. But if you refuse to forgive others, your Father will not forgive your sins." [3] So, today, we can begin the process of forgiving our earthly mums and dads, and letting go of the anger, the hurt, mistreatment or even abuse that have been caused in the past.

Alongside forgiveness comes the need to take responsibility and to say sorry for our negative reactions towards those who have wronged us. Have you had the heart of a son or daughter

---

3   Matthew 6:14,15 NLT

towards your earthly fathers? Just as you weren't fathered in the way you should have been, so you can also repent for not being the son or daughter to your parents and for your rejecting them. At some point we chose not to be a son or daughter to our earthly mum or dad, so, as we say sorry, we are released and return to the security of being a child of our heavenly Dad.

It is only through truly forgiving that the cycle is broken. Even if we have been sinned against and treated wrongly, through forgiveness the blockages are removed, and this releases God to deal with the offender. We no longer carry the deep bitterness and pain of unforgiveness. When we withhold forgiveness, we are the one suffering by punishing ourselves. God can only bring conviction in the life of another person if we forgive and allow God to do His work.

It takes time to look honestly at the state of our hearts, and allow a softening to begin. As the eyes of our heart are opened to the revelation of the Father's love, so we recognize our own orphan-mindedness, our fear, shame and low self-esteem. When we get to the place of acknowledging and uncovering our own self-condemnation and deep pain, we are able to forgive, and see ourselves as God the Father sees us. Receiving the Father's love unblocks emotional pain due to failed relationships from the past. We are alive, uncluttered, and hungry for more love.

John's Gospel is full of the truth that points to God as Father, and reading this stirs up the desire to know God intimately as our Father, the Dad we never knew. John the disciple stayed close to Jesus physically and in doing so received revelation of the Father. As we nurture our relationship with Jesus, we are drawn closer to God as Father. The past that tried to mould us no longer defines us as we are released from past rejection and pain. As we wrap ourselves in the love of a Father who is trustworthy and thank God that the abuse and betrayal of the past no longer define us, we are loosed from the deep roots of our past and come to life. Faith grows.

Jesus says, *"But remember to forgive. You can forgive, because I have forgiven you. No-one is perfect; all have missed the mark. Forgiveness is the key to restoration and renewing your mind. Keep on forgiving whenever negative thoughts surface. Forgiveness is a way of life, and the quicker you get into the habit, the better. Practise forgiveness. Follow My example of forgiveness. I forgave a hurting world, because they did not know what they were doing. Hurting people hurt others. The only way for the cycle to be broken is by forgiving. And you can only forgive because I first forgave you. I have taken the initiative. From the cross I forgave, in order to open the floodgates of forgiveness. I said 'Father, forgive them, for they do not know what they do.'* [4] *I forgive, so you now are able to forgive. The spirit of forgiveness comes from Me. Those who don't know Me find it hard to forgive, but relationship with Me begins with receiving My forgiveness. Forgiveness is the fertile ground for relationship, the good soil in which life grows."*

---

4   Luke 23:34

Conclusion

When the apostle Paul was in Athens he noticed an inscription with the words, "To the Unknown God". He spoke to the council there about it, and he could be saying the same thing about people today!

"I notice that you are very religious in every way, for as I was walking along I saw your many shrines … This God, whom you worship without knowing, is the one I'm telling you about. He is the God who made the world and everything in it. Since he is Lord of heaven and earth, he doesn't live in man-made temples … He himself gives life and breath to everything, and he satisfies every need. From one man he created all the nations throughout the whole earth … His purpose was for the nations to seek after God and perhaps feel their way toward him and find him – though he is not far from any one of us. For in him we live and move and exist. As some of your own poets have said, 'We are His offspring.'" [1]

When you were born, your life was a blank page, unspoiled, pure. God began writing on the page, even before you entered the world. He wrote words of truth on your page, deep truths engraved into you. Truth has been there from the foundation of the world; before you were conceived, you were known by Him. You were called, you were chosen, you were predestined as a child of God. He knew every fibre of your being; He is

---

1   Acts 17:22-28 NLT

intimately acquainted with the cells in your body. You are unique. He created you as a master craftsman creates His work. Creativity is who He is – you are special, you are unique, nothing compares with you. God delighted in you before you were born, before you took your first breath. Never doubt your uniqueness. You are so important to Him. Just as an artist delights in creativity, so He delights in you; creativity is perfection. Your life has been a journey with Him, as He has held you. As a perfect Mother and Father, He will never leave you, and never neglects you. He has never left you. When times are dark, He is closest to you. Don't despise hard times – these are His special moments with you. Treasure this time. Your birth rocked heaven!

God is saying, "I am your true Father, the Father of fathers. I am your perfect Father; I am trustworthy. I won't let you down. As you forgive your earthly father, a mere shadow of fatherhood, I am filling your life with the true Father's love. A child knows Me in a way they don't know their earthly father. I am always with you when you are alone. I promise never to leave you. You are no longer an orphan. I am untangling previous loss, shame, guilt, self-doubt, affirming you as my child, my son, my daughter. The prodigals are coming home, to where they belong."

Rather than this being the end of the book, it is the beginning. The journey of discovery has just started; a challenge to keep seeking the Father. Now is the time to ask Jesus to "show us the Father". As we do this, Jesus gives the same response as He did Philip, "He who has seen Me, has seen the Father." [2]

---

2   John 14:9

Bibliography

The Concise Oxford Dictionary (1974). Oxford University Press: Ely House, London, UK.

Arnott, J (1995) *The Father's Blessing.* Creation House, Strang Communications Company: Orlando, FL, USA.

Cambridge Dictionary (2010) Cambridge University Press: Cambridge, UK.

Hamon, Dr B (2010) *Prophetic Scriptures yet to be Fulfilled.* Destiny Image Publishers, Inc: Shippensburg, PA, USA.

Hamon, Dr B (2019) *Your Highest Calling.* Chosen Books, Baker Publishing Group: Grand Rapids, Michigan, USA.

Howell, E. (2018) *How Many Stars Are in the Universe?* Available at www.space.com (2021).

Capper, W.M. (1954) *Arthur Rendle Short: Surgeon and Christian.* Inter-varsity Fellowship: London, UK.

Button, L (2009) *Father Matter.* HPS Publishing: Essex, UK.

Hayward, C (2019) *The End of Rejection.* Regal Books and Chosen Books: USA.

Goll, J.W. (2021) *The Feeler.* Whitaker House: 1030 Hunt Valley Circle, New Kensington, PA, USA.

Fujimura, M. (2020) *A Theology of Making, Art and Faith.* University Press: Yale, New Haven & London, UK.

Jordan, J (2012) *Sonship, A Journey into Father's Heart.* Father heart Media: Taupo, New Zealand.

Rendle Short, A. (1956) *The Diary of George Muller: Selected Extracts.* Pickering & Inglis Ltd: London, UK.

Verrynne, A. (2022) *A Compass for the Heart.* Oxygen Life Church, 13 Second Avenue, Walmer, Port Elizabeth, South Africa.

Williamson, G.I. (2003) *The Westminster Shorter Catechism*, Presbyterian and Reformed; First Edition.

Printed in Great Britain
by Amazon

23794285R00067